AD EXITUS

One Person's Perspective on Humanity
and Its Future

by
J. Frank Sexton

1st Edition, February 2012

This edition is also available in e-book format

Cover design by J. F. Sexton

The image, taken from space, is a sunset over
North America

ISBN: 978-0-9878820-4-2

Dedication

This book is dedicated to those who often stop to think but seldom have the time to commit their thoughts to writing. Take heart and make the time. Your thoughts belong to you but have value only when shared.

And for teaching me the value of just doing something without thought once in a while, this book is also dedicated to my life partner **Robert (Bobby)** who has put up with my passionate pursuit of perfection for more than 30 years.

Acknowledgements

For giving me the time and encouragement to articulate my ideas about the workplace, I would like to thank **S.B.**, **W.G.** and **G.A.** all of whom were senior executives in the Canadian civil service and my boss at one time or another. While none of them should be blamed for anything presented here, all of them allowed me the room to think and grow.

Prologue

Why did I write this book?

I have had a rather bland and uneventful life, at least as measured against the people whose names appear regularly in our media and classrooms. I am not famous, although I am known to a lot of people. I am not powerful, although I have influenced many. I am not inventive, although I have often drawn upon the knowledge of others to present different alternatives. And I am certainly not rich, although I have never really wanted for anything important to me.

But like just about everyone I have ever known, I have often thought about our planet and that thinking has been influenced by the people and events in my life. Furthermore, I believe that my thoughts, like other people's thoughts in a free society, deserve to be expressed for better or worse.

I wanted to put down on paper both my observations on life and my own history that influenced those thoughts. There have been so many things that have happened in my life to which I attribute some influence that I feared forgetting to mention them here. To understand something always involves more than just observing its current condition, and that is why it is important that parts of my own life be documented.

As I was writing, memories of people and events came flooding back. Some of those were good, some not so good. The purpose of this effort was not, however, to be an autobiography. It was to express my perspective on a variety of issues and offer some alternatives.

Most of the topics I have written about are fundamental to life and affect virtually everyone on this planet. Whether I have succeeded in adding to humanity's understanding of those issues is for you, the reader, to decide. This is not an attempt to be an academic work driven by research and study, but rather a thoughtful expression of what I have observed, my assessment of those things and, based on that, some suggestions for the future.

A good friend who read some early drafts of this book thought it reflected elements of Ayn Rand's philosophy of Objectivism. In a moment of false pride I had assumed that many of my ideas were original but his allusion to the author of "Atlas Shrugged" made me scramble to investigate. I had never read any of Ayn Rand's works and had honestly not heard of Objectivism. But a very quick search on the Internet yielded considerable evidence that my outlook on life bears some affinity to the Objectivist perspective. I can truthfully say that I arrived at the conclusions presented here by my own devices, but there are, nevertheless, similarities which must be acknowledged.

I consider logic and observation to be essential to human existence. I am an atheist, although I am fascinated with the diverse religions on this planet and their sometimes contrasting, sometimes complimentary, dogmas. I do not believe in violence against other human beings, although I acknowledge that it exists either as a threat to enforce compliance with some idea or person, or as a reality in war, criminal action and social punishment.

But there are also differences.

I am certainly not a *laissez-faire* capitalist because the drive to create wealth is always at the expense of someone else in society. Money is a notional concept, the value of which is based on the products and services created in a given economy. Unless the real economy expands at a pace greater than inflation, the exchange of money is a zero-sum game with one entity paying and another being paid. With easy credit, it is possible to pay out much more than income received but that cannot continue indefinitely because it will eventually, whether for individual, corporation or country, create economic catastrophe. But money, once paid out, cannot be re-used for other things and it remains a moot point whether the goods or services received in exchange for money are truly equal.

I do not believe in the absolute rights of the individual as they are expressed today but rather in a negotiated truce between human beings. Such a truce ought to respect everyone's basic needs to breathe, to drink, to eat and to be sheltered from the elements. It also ought to respect their need to think, to express those thoughts and to learn of others' thoughts. Furthermore, it ought to ensure that the resources of this finite planet will be shared equitably, not squandered through waste and pollution, and not be exhausted through greed. No one should be prevented from pursuing any physical activity if that activity does not violate the terms of this negotiated truce. The only restriction on the freedom of activity would be the requirement for informed consent when it involves two or more human beings. An offence to the senses should not be something to be sanctioned or prevented. In fact, exposure to the greatest possible diversity of sights, smells, sounds and tastes ought to promote the greatest tolerance, acceptance and even assimilation of those differences.

Two of the greatest forces at work on this planet are evolution and adaptation. When something does not work, or does not work well, it inevitably evolves to something else or ceases to exist. Since nothing in our world has been found to be perfect, everything eventually ends and is sometimes replaced, often with something better, sometimes not. There is no reason to think that humanity is an exception. Only by encouraging the sharing, and even the assimilation, of differences, can humanity hope to master these forces rather than nature randomly deciding our future.

All living things are motivated by self-interest, and when that self-interest is complimentary or supplementary to the self-interest of other living things, then the entire ecosystem becomes harmonious and self-perpetuating. But when the self-interest of one is contrary to the self-interest of another, then potentially one gains while the other is diminished. When there are too many winners and losers at too rapid a pace, it can ultimately lead to the extinction of all. Such an extinction would be the result of the gossamer threads of interdependence between living things being destroyed faster than they can be replaced.

So what do I call myself and my philosophical observations? I doubt that any single label would best describe me. I am the same as every other person on this planet, unique. I am the product of biology and my interactions with many people and events.

All too often people tend to focus on things and events that support their own way of thinking and tend to dismiss or rationalize things and events that do not. From religious leaders who interpret everything as proving their own dogma to politicians who take credit for the good and lay blame for the bad, everyone has difficulty treating reality objectively. While I have tried to escape my own bias and background, that is not always possible. For example, I continue to hope that humanity will change and improve its behaviour but deep inside I believe that it is impossible. My own hopes cloud my logic. But that is all the more reason to include my history so that the reader may know what has influenced me.

My conclusions on humanity and life in general are a result of my upbringing, my working career and my earnest attempts to listen, learn and objectively assess new things. That does not mean an end to dialogue since I believe that truth is the most elusive of objectives and therefore I do not presume to think that what I have concluded is absolute and true.

The brief and selected narrative about my life will show that I am not an ivory tower academic who has never been in the workplace to earn a living. While I did earn a graduate degree, I rose from a working class background as an assembly line worker to computer programmer to managing projects worth many millions of dollars. I have visited every province in my country, have friends in many of those provinces, and have lived in three of them. I have visited a number of other countries physically and visited many more virtually. With every step, I learned something new about me and about the world around me.

I ended my salaried career as one of the thousands of anonymous bureaucrats who administer the laws and regulations of my country. Every bureaucrat has a function in the running of a country whether that function is big or small. Bureaucrats do the work that citizens demand through their politicians who, in turn, enact laws and regulations to satisfy those demands. Early in my country's history, to avoid corruption and nepotism, politicians established an arm's length Commission to hire public servants who could work in absolute neutrality. Nevertheless, every single bureaucrat is doing the will of some citizen or citizens. While these same citizens may feel that there are many tasks being performed by the civil service that are not needed and, in fact, are a waste of money, each and every law and regulation is a result of one or more citizens asking that it be done.

But civil servants are not unthinking machines. There are many who have strongly held opinions about society and its governance. They think about people and the planet and they care. In an odd and sometimes cruel irony, it is only their job that prevents them from doing anything other than administering the law as it stands. And the law can be a cold and unyielding master.

I have always had deep thoughts about people and the world around us. But I could never express such thoughts because I was committed to serving my country as required by the government of the day. However, now that I have retired, I have the freedom to share my thoughts with anyone who might care to listen and I have tried to do so in this book.

Inside these pages, I have mused about the nature of good and evil and how both fear and hope influence all of us. I have also raised issues about life and the universe around us. I have even pondered why conflict continues to exist between humans on a massive scale.

I have already briefly explained my position on human rights earlier in this prologue, but in the book I have tried to explain how I arrived at those conclusions and then offer an entirely different notion of rights. I hope you will think about the consequences of so fundamental a change and what it would mean to you and those around you.

On a more practical level, I have documented my observations on male sexuality. The male of our species constantly craves satisfaction, but then builds obstacles to realizing it. I do not believe this contradiction is based solely on any moral conviction so I have proposed a different thesis. If true, it would also explain why there has been such antipathy between straight and gay men for so many centuries

No one likes to be taxed. But the unfairness of virtually all systems of taxation actively encourages this dislike. Further, government spending of our money in practically every country seems to be out of control. Therefore, I have proposed an entirely new model for both taxation and governmental expenditures. I hope that my rather radical suggestions will trigger at least some discussion.

And to help others feel empowered to express their ideas, I have added a discussion of truth, knowledge and wisdom. It is important to realize that even though everyone else believes something that does not make it true. The thought of encouraging even one mind to overcome shyness and put down on paper something new that moves our understanding forward would be wonderful.

For my part, I fully realize that most of my suggestions will never be implemented, but that does not make them invalid. However, if one believes in an idea then it is important to express it. And to turn an idea into reality, one must understand human behaviour and apply that understanding to give change a chance. Therefore, I have also noted some key principles about human behaviour that I believe are critical to know when dealing with those around us and changing their opinions.

While the other things about which I have written in this book are important, I have saved the most important topic for the end. I have a deep concern about the future of our species. Humanity continues to expand and consume ever greater resources without any long term understanding of the consequences of doing so. Therefore, I have identified the five critical issues that, in my opinion, must be addressed for our continued well-being and even our very existence. For each of those issues, I have offered a potential solution. Whether those suggestions, or other better ideas inspired by them, will ever be realized remains for the future to decide. But I believe that failure to address these issues in some manner means our ultimate failure as a species.

I have allowed myself a rather unusual vanity by introducing each chapter with a quote. Quoting someone is not odd in itself, but these quotes come from myself. Each one represents something fundamental to my outlook recorded in as few words as possible.

So sit back, relax, and open your mind to my observations and assessments of people and life. I hope you will feel amused, perplexed, outraged or challenged but never bored. I also hope that this work will encourage you to really take the time to think and perhaps commit your own thoughts to paper as I have done.

One last thing, if you like this book, please suggest to a friend that they buy a copy, or better yet, buy a copy for them. This entire effort has been without the benefit of an editor, publisher or marketing agent. I count on you, the reader, to be both my advertiser and patron. I do not expect to sell a million copies or get rich by this effort, but it would be gratifying to know that there were at least some people who read and enjoyed my work whether or not they agreed with it. That is all any writer can ask.

J. Frank Sexton

Table of Contents

Part 1: 1952 to 1979

1) Overture

"The growth of human knowledge is almost always impeded by that which we know to be certain today."

J. F. Sexton

To continuously hear scientists describe Earth as perfectly suited to life is to hear echoes of the ancient belief that the Earth was the centre of the universe. Humans have only just barely moved from that self-centered bias despite centuries of advancement.

If the relationship of life to Earth is stated in reverse, in other words, that Earth's life evolved based upon the conditions present on Earth during Earth's own evolution as a member of this stellar system, then it is possible to imagine life existing in many forms across the universe based on the environment in which each species arose.

Earthly life is perfectly suited to this planet's conditions simply because that particular type of life evolved here. That is probably the reason that life can be found almost everywhere on this planet.

Because of humanity's biased perceptions, until recently it was thought there could not be any life elsewhere in this solar system. But observations have indicated that life may exist, or have existed, in a number of places other than Earth. That idea, if it had been expressed only 500 years ago, would have resulted in arrest by religious zealots and possible execution for heresy. Galileo came close to that fate simply for expressing the idea that the Earth was not the centre of the universe.

Stepping outside of the human experience or humanity's assumptions to document them objectively has often been dangerous and always puts the observer in a small minority, viewed at best as quirky.

But having full knowledge of the risk, here are more observations about humans.

By definition, humans are parasites on this planet, engorging themselves on the resources that are readily available and giving back little in return. With the exception of sky burials in the Himalayas, most humans even try to protect their bodies after death, thereby blocking the planet's natural recycling. And like all parasites, humans risk consuming all the resources of their host and thereby killing it and themselves at the same time.

Homo sapiens did not exist as a species 200,000 years ago, a time span which represents a mere 0.00015% of the universe's approximately 14 billion years. Of course, that estimate of the universe's age is only a calculation based on today's assumptions and, in fact, the universe may be much older, much younger or even of infinite age. Regardless, this young species has shown itself in that short time to be a deadly and voracious mutation evolved to be more destructive than any other species in Earth's history. Their brains and physical capabilities allow them to adapt to just about any adverse condition in nature. Because of their growth and spread, they have become immune, as a species, from just about any natural disaster, such as famine, plague, or weather. And like any deadly parasite, humans seem to be helpless to do anything more than what they have evolved to do.

It is based upon this fundamental observation concerning humanity that the title of this book was selected. *Ad exitus* is a Latin phrase which can be interpreted many ways. Among its meanings are "going out" and "going forth". And at this point in time, it is unclear which definition might apply to humanity and its future. It is unclear if humanity is headed out of existence or if it can go forth to profitably co-exist with all life on this planet including its own kind.

* * *

Regardless of what tomorrow brings, all humans, including myself, hope for a better future.

Therefore, this is a good place to begin introducing you, dear reader, to my rather boring life and my thoughts and observations about life which I hope are anything but boring.

I have alternated a history of my own life which includes many observations and conclusions about human behaviour, with short essays on, for example, life, truth, society, money, conflict and sex. These essays are drawn from my own experiences and, when put together, paint a perspective of humanity that may not be entirely unique but is uniquely mine.

I have always lived by a set of rules and one of the most important of those is to say nothing if either I agree with everyone else (thereby adding a redundant voice to an already noisy planet) or if I disagree with everyone but cannot propose any alternative. Criticism can never be constructive unless it includes a reasonable alternative, something I wish every chronic complainer would remember. While the essays included here are not meant as criticisms of humanity, I recognize that there is always value in offering alternatives even if these choices are unlikely ever to be selected. Therefore where possible, I have made suggestions designed to lessen the problems of this planet despite knowing that many readers will think them naive or impossible.

But if you believe these ideas are impossible, stop a moment to remember the certainties of the past before reaching that conclusion. Remember when the Earth was the centre of the universe? Remember when it was flat? More recently, remember when the speed of light was the maximum possible speed? It looks more and more like Einstein got it wrong.

In addition, you will get a glimpse of one bureaucrat's life within the civil service. I hope you will be pleasantly surprised by the internal workings of my country's administration. You will also see the other side of a bureaucrat, the private side, a side that does not really fit the stereotype.

Is all the history presented here accurate as best I can remember it? Yes. Is everything here my own honest opinion based on the facts I have observed throughout my life? Yes. Do I believe everything that I have written is the absolute truth and the end of dialogue? Certainly not. I do not believe that truth is something easily or ever attained. What is obvious today is ignorance and stupidity tomorrow.

But if you disagree with whatever I have written, please do so in civil discourse which is one of the hallmarks of intellectual endeavour. Debate is much better than simple denial when that denial is based solely upon today's understandings.

2) Good & Evil

"Normal is a fictional notion used to denigrate others."

J. F. Sexton

When someone observes another person and notes that the other person's looks or behaviour are "not normal", they are making a negative comparison to some idealized standard that may exist only in their imagination. Such conclusions are always fraught with danger, being coloured by the perception of what "normal" is. In fact, many standards of appearance and behaviour can hardly be called absolute since they change with the passage of time.

Having said that, there are probably some things that represent absolute good and other things that represent absolute evil, but what are they?

Is it wrong to kill? This is an absolute statement that, if true, would morally condemn millions of people who believed themselves to have been acting on the side of good during times of war. Those in power go to great lengths to find moral justification for the act of killing people, both in times of war and in times of peace. The powerful do so in order that those who commit the acts on their behalf can rationalize killing other human beings despite being taught that such acts are evil. But do the Ten Commandments given to Moses include an exception clause to the "thou shalt not kill" rule?

What is the ultimate good? Is it love, charity, kindness, or something else? Can an emotion be good or can good only be expressed in an act? It is doubtful that a hermit having no contact with other humans for many years can be categorized as either good or evil since there is no one against which to measure the hermit's actions.

Therefore, good and evil can only be thought of as attributes of acts that take place between two entities. It is never something that can be attributed in isolation. To attribute good to a person, that person must have demonstrated an overwhelming propensity to do good things for others.

Should good be measured by the motive of the act? Motive is

probably an important factor in measuring the goodness of an act, but knowing the motives of another is never truly possible. Motive really does not matter to those directly involved in the act, but makes a difference to those who observe it. If knowing an act of goodness may be interpreted by others as making the giver of the act good, then is the giver actually motivated by self-promotion? In other words, is the giver motivated by selfish aggrandizement, rather than altruism? Politicians routinely use the photo-opportunity to convey their goodness, but their motive is probably not as altruistic as they would like the rest of the world to believe.

Can good acts be prioritized, that is, can good be owed to one person and denied to another at the same time and still be good? There are obvious genetic reasons for choosing good with respect to one's biological relations and denying it to others, but are there times when doing good for the species must be preferred over doing good for one's own gene pool? And what about doing good for the planet over the species? Would anyone seriously expect a world leader to put planet over citizens, or species?

Should good be measured against the social expectations of the day, or is it something that transcends time? Would Christian society praise someone who burned a heretic today? Can any form of punishment be considered good when, if taken out of context, it would be considered evil? Most societies would recoil in horror at the actions of our ancestors only a few centuries ago. Take execution by being "hung, drawn and quartered" which was carried out in full public view as righteous retribution for some heinous act. The convicted were strangled until half-conscious thereby rendering them less susceptible to losing complete awareness of what was to come. Then they had their genitals cut off and burned before their eyes. Following that, their belly was opened, their bowels pulled out and also burned. Finally, and one must presume to the great relief of the condemned, they died as their head was cut off. Is there anyone today that would seriously advocate this form of punishment? It is more likely that a strong consensus would cry out at the evil of this act.

Free societies operate on the basis that anything not proscribed by the rules (or laws) is good, or at least acceptable, while ordered societies operate on the basis that good is defined by the rules and they are the only acts permitted. Free societies constantly invent new rules to deem specific acts evil while ordered societies constantly invent new rules to deem acts good. Is either type of society inherently good or evil? It is rather superficial to categorize an entire society as either good or evil. Instead, it is more appropriate to attribute good or evil to the powerful who dictate and enforce the rules in a society.

It may surprise most people that good and evil are so slippery a concept. They are slippery because their definitions change over time and they are often measured by moral beliefs that differ from one society to the next. Like pornography, most people claim to know what good and evil are but when forced to define them fall short or fall awry of their neighbour's definition.

When one is a child, the difference between good and evil is defined by one's parents. And those definitions are accepted as simple truth. As one matures, the inevitable questions start to arise about things that are close to the margins of either side. And as one ages, it no longer stays the simplistic black and white world that one enjoyed in youth. Such is the loss of innocence.

The simple question of good and evil is perhaps the best example of why everything ought to be questioned and why truth is so elusive. It is also the best example of why words having even less weight, like "normal", can be so abused and hurtful.

3) My Early Life

"You are the result of what you are made from and moulded by. It is the combination of those two things that makes each person unique."

J. F. Sexton

A Gesture To Those I Have Known

Everything that I consider important or influential in my life that I can remember or that I have discovered, I have tried to write down in this work. I have always had a terrible memory for names and so, despite real names popping up in my brain from time to time, I have made a conscious effort not to use them here. That is not an effort to protect the guilty, just an effort to ensure that no one feels an obligation to either support or dispute what I have recorded. If people recognize themselves, then it is up to them to decide to remain anonymous or not. I have no quarrel with either decision. All names are important to their owners, but history really only cares about ideas and actions, noting the vanity of those who would have their names remembered forever.

Some of the actions I will describe may illicit demands for more details particularly by those who may feel that they ought to do something about what happened or prevent similar things from happening in the future. I will not answer those demands since my purpose here is simply to outline my life's experiences, setting the stage on which I have developed my thoughts. It is a matter of inner peace to disclose the facts. It is revenge to want identities known. If there are some that wish to do the research to determine the names associated with some of the events I have described, I would wish they not do so. There is no one to be found from my past that is either rich or famous to be torn down by those seeking their own fame. I do not believe there is anyone in my past that should feel guilt because of what they did since I believe they all acted in accordance with their beliefs at the time.

My Family Background and First Years

I have a number of disjointed and dateless memories that predate my first years at school.

Despite where I grew up in Chatham, deep in South-Western Ontario, I have fond memories of the huge snow bank that would grow beside our back steps. In retrospect, it could not have been more than a foot or so tall, but to a little tyke, it was a mountain to be jumped over or squashed.

One summer, I found a really large black and yellow spider in one of the basement windows. It fascinated me and to properly observe it, I captured flies in our screen windows and fed them to the spider. It was amazing to watch this predator either consume them or wrap them up for later.

My father tried valiantly to create a backyard skating rink several years in a row. But when he finally figured out that the only things needing sharpening were my ankles rather than the blades on my skates, he quietly gave up on my budding NHL career.

I never knew either my paternal or maternal grandparents. They all passed away either before I was born or before I was old enough to remember anything of them. But I was truly emotionally struck when I discovered that both my father's parents passed away within five weeks of each other in 1944 when he and my uncle, his younger brother, were overseas serving as volunteers in the army. I do not think I can begin to understand how this must have felt to be so far away when both his parents were taken.

The heritage of both my mother's and father's families was apparent quite early and reflected in the huge garden that my father kept. Many of my mother's family were farmers and my father's dad was a horticulturist when he immigrated from England bringing my dad as a small babe. While I never set out to learn about growing things, I continue to surprise myself by recalling important details about how to plant and harvest the diverse things that my dad grew. The far back of the lot contained three apple trees, two pear trees, a plum tree, a sour cherry tree and a peach tree. There was also a grape vine which never really produced well despite the yearly spring optimism. In the garden proper, there were raspberry canes, strawberry vines, red and black current bushes, rhubarb bushes plus a wide variety of vegetables including the basics like spinach, sweet peas, sweet corn, cabbage, turnips, squash, parsnips, carrots, tomatoes and the odd experiment with lettuce and cauliflower. Two crops, almost always tried and almost always failed, were watermelon and cantaloupe (or musk melon, as my dad called them). The cantaloupe vines usually produced at least a few melons that could be savoured when they ripened but the watermelon patch rarely worked.

The most enduring and pleasant memories of that garden and orchard were the tastes. I took those things for granted until I left home and had to start buying them from local grocery stores. I never truly appreciated the incredible flavours of real fresh and ripe produce until I could not find them. Stores may label things as fresh or vine ripened, but a tomato that is hard or crunchy is not as it should be, sweet and juicy and firm but yielding.

Dad would spend endless summer evenings talking with one neighbour in particular, arguing over some special techniques to increase the yields or make things plumper, juicier or sweeter. I always thought they were in a fierce race to determine who was the better gardener but I can see now they were just enjoying the challenge together.

The family also ventured out on Sunday drives to harvest some of the wild things that grew outside the city. We hunted for wild asparagus that grew along some ditches. There were also wooded areas where we found morels, an edible variety of fungus.

Dad was also an avid fisherman who would spend what time he could in both summer and winter catching what he could, cleaning it and then freezing it for later consumption.

I also hung around my mom as she went through the annual routine of canning this, freezing that, making jam or jelly or even waxing turnips. I have often surprised myself by recalling the fine details of her technique and I think I could do what she did even now, assuming I could work up the energy. The one thing that she did from time to time that I would not dare do myself today is to bake bread from scratch. It was a full day's labour and took strong arms to kneed and roll the dough. Even she marvelled at how her ancestors could have baked all their own bread each and every week.

I remember playing with the two boys next door, one of whom was slightly older and the other slightly younger. They were both blond and I envied their athletic skills and confidence. As most boys that age do, we explored the neighbourhood and with evil intent scooped up fruit and other goodies that had strayed from their trees or vines in distant backyards. However, I just never got the proper hang of innocently picking up some apple or whatever and then explaining how it could not have come from the tree standing next to me. So I just let my friends have their fun. I did, however, discover that it was fun to play with the little girl across the street. That came to a somewhat abrupt halt when mom decreed that it wasn't right to be playing alone in the basement with her.

Quite a few things were different in those days. The way people interacted within a neighbourhood is a prime example. Doors were not locked or locked only when no one was home for an extended period. Friends and neighbours never used the front door, and always rapped, not knocked, at the back door before entering. Thinking back, every neighbour had a unique knock that identified them before they even shouted hello. The front door was reserved for relatives and other important visitors. Children, like myself, were generally banned from living rooms and dining rooms for fear of creating a mess that would look bad if important company arrived unexpectedly. The kitchen, basement, our bedrooms and the great outdoors were our domain.

For most of these early years, my dad was away during the week working for a company building highways and was only home on the weekends. Neither he nor my mother completed more than the 10th and 8th grade respectively, but my dad had an uncanny ability to do complex arithmetic in his head. He could also visualize products from drawings and could pinpoint weaknesses in design or proposed construction before cutting the first piece of steel or pouring the first square yard of concrete. When he changed jobs and worked in a local tool and die shop, those abilities were put to good use.

I believe I inherited my father's ability to work out problems in his head and to conceptualize solutions without going through a process of trial and error. This is not something that can be learned or acquired through training. I often saw him pause to mentally go through a process, solving problems before they even appeared. While his world was simpler, I really believe that he was far more intelligent than he admitted even to himself. I remember feeling badly when, because of his lack of a formal education, I sometimes witnessed his embarrassment not knowing the correct word he wanted to use.

I also believe that my father inherited a sense of deference from his family who immigrated to Canada from England in 1913. I saw it but simply accepted it as normal. In an academic sense, I better understand it today but I cannot say that I escaped its effects.

He was born in England but was just a small babe when his family sought new roots in the vastness of the Dominion of Canada. Being born in England and carrying the rights of a UK citizen did not seem important to him but being Canadian did. When the government announced new rules which required folks like him to request citizenship a couple of decades after he fought for Canada in the Second World War, he was as angry as I had ever seen him. Although it was only an administrative technicality, he proclaimed himself a proud Canadian who did not need any bureaucrat to confirm it.

This was just one example of his strong sense of what was right and wrong. He also believed in what worked and what did not, and had an endless curiosity about how things were done. All of those things influenced me much more than I realized at the time.

I had a sister that I never knew. Like so many of their generation, the Second World War interrupted my parents' lives. They got married before my dad left to go overseas but when it was over they moved to the big city, Chatham. My sister was born in 1946 as part of the first wave of the baby boom after the war.

I found a book recently, given to my mother to keep track of the new arrival's milestones. In her impeccable handwriting, she noted the baby's first words, when they were spoken, how tall and big she was getting on each birthday, and even the presents she received from friends and relatives. The book was structured to keep track of the first five years and the first four years were filled with proud moments.

But my sister died suddenly before reaching her fifth birthday and her death was always a mystery to me before reading this book. It was a subject spoken only in whispers in an attempt, no doubt, to soften what must have been a terrible event in my mother's life and to spare me from becoming aware of this dark and painful chapter. I only knew that my sister had become ill and was taken to hospital where she died that night. Today, with the help of my mother's own writing, I know that my sister succumbed to influenza. The flu has always been a threat to the young and the old and many still perish from it today, but it was a surprise to me to discover this about my sister. It also goes a long way in explaining my mother's constant attention to my health and diet.

The family went to the Detroit Zoo with my mother's youngest brother and his wife every summer. It was something that I remember with enormous fondness. It was exotic and exciting. But one summer, those trips ceased. It was a hard blow to take but I remember being told something vague about not wanting to be there since the crowd had changed. I think this was my first encounter with racism. I simply did not understand but, like most children, I accepted what I was told.

Later during a visit by my mother's oldest sister, a widow the second time by then, the three of us went downtown to the Eaton's store. That in itself was a special treat because the store had an elevator, operated by a very nice lady. I always looked forward to at least one trip on that elevator whether it was to go up or down. When my mother left me with her sister to look for something in lady's wear that was not appropriate for a boy to be looking at, a couple entered the store and walked by. I did not notice anything unusual until my aunt leaned over and quietly whispered in my ear that he "should know better and keep to his own kind". The couple was a young black man and a young white woman. I still did not quite understand although I look back now with sadness at that incident. I cannot be angry with my aunt because she was a reflection of her times.

Did I mention that the elevator operator was a black woman?

Chatham had a small black population and there were other towns not far from Chatham that were almost exclusively black, like North Buxton. The famous baseball player, Ferguson Jenkins, grew up in the African-Canadian community in Chatham. I now know that this area was a northern terminus of the underground railroad and that is how these communities were created. The historic site of "Uncle Tom's Cabin" rests about 20 minutes drive from Chatham.

But at that moment, I was simply curious about what my aunt

had said. It did not seem logical but she was old and understood things better than me.

4) Fear

"People can and do change, but that evolution is often based on a bedrock belief and value system that is far less likely to evolve."

J. F. Sexton

It is often said that one cannot teach an old dog new tricks. That is nonsense. An old dog is difficult to train simply because it lacks motivation. It calculates what is to be gained by behaving in some new manner. In its youth, those tasty treats were enough, but now rest and sunny skies satisfy more than behaving in some strange manner for a small morsel.

It is similar with people. People do change and learn new things throughout their lives but they often measure each opportunity by some fundamental standard that they learned in their youth. If that change conflicts with their fundamental beliefs they are much less likely to gladly embrace it.

Emotions are fundamental to human life. As such, challenging an emotional reaction is a very difficult thing to do at any age.

Fear is one of the most basic of human emotions. It is, no doubt, a defence mechanism which prevents humans from doing themselves serious harm. Fear is the word that humans use to describe the brain's commands to various parts of the body to prepare to fight or flee in case of real danger. The adrenaline flows, the body's temperature rises reflecting increased energy consumption by the muscles, and all the senses become focused on providing information to the brain so it can make the call to fight or flee.

Fear is generated by many things, principle among them is the unknown. When one is lost and hungry, those red ripe berries look enticing but there is hesitation because fear has kicked in based on the uncertainty of the consequences of eating some unknown fruit. Without fear, humans would have failed as a species many millennia ago.

The greatest fear is generated by the perceived uncertainty of life itself. For those who know their fate, such as a patient in the final stages of terminal cancer, fear disappears. It disappears once there is nothing left unknown or uncertain. Fear disappears, replaced by an unnatural calm, in the soldier who knows that death is a certain outcome in the coming minutes. Many suicides present the same unnatural calm because uncertainty has departed.

But when hope remains, fear is its inevitable companion.

Even the swaggering soul who bravely performs tasks which strike fear into everyone else, has fear but has learned that there are rewards for sublimating that fear with bravado. Humans tend to reward others who can seemingly bury their fear and perform feats that would not otherwise be done by "normal" people. However, the future is seldom bright for humans whose learning years are filled with rewards for doing things others would not, since they will often continue to seek those rewards by ever more risky behaviour. Rolling the dice too often is a recipe for deadly failure.

But fear caused by the unknown can also find expression in some ugly behaviour. Fear of someone who is different is caused by ignorance. When that person is known, logical decisions can be made about whether that individual is a friend or foe and thus fear disappears. But that same fear of a person who is different can sometimes be transferred to all persons who appear to have the same difference. That is the basis for racism and all other forms of xenophobia so prevalent in the world today.

A fundamental error of logic is committed when a bad experience with one individual is deemed to be the likely outcome when dealing with any and all similar looking or acting persons. And yet, humans fall into this trap regularly.

To examine why this is so, one need only to go back to the experience of being lost in the woods. An unknown berry might be poisonous so humans avoid eating it. But if a berry of a recognized species is found, it is eaten. That known berry will taste different from other berries on the same bush due to differences in age, sunlight and even droppings from passing birds. But it is still fundamentally a nutritious berry. Later on, it might be learned that the unknown berry was even more nutritious but suspicion remains until the berry can actually be tasted. Once sampled and found to be delicious, other berries of the same species can be enjoyed until a particularly sour one is found. That one sour berry can permanently change a person's taste for that fruit. Logic should, but often does not, intervene to say that one berry does not represent the norm.

Fear, particularly of the unknown, has also been used by some humans to take advantage of others. The simplest example today is the salesman who manipulates a person's fear of the unknown to obtain money in return for a guarantee to prevent some event or to compensate if that event happens despite the guarantees. But throughout history, fear has been used to gain more than just money. Fear is a potent emotion that can be manipulated by individuals who claim they can eliminate fear's cause if they are given the power to do so. It is hard to think of any dictator in history that has not promised to shield the people from some fearful danger.

Fear can also be created where none existed before. Marketing regularly instills the fear of being the "last one on the block...". Politicians regularly instill fear of what their opponents might do. To reject these messages requires the courage of one's convictions and a sound knowledge base. Knowledge almost always roles back fear, often replacing it with strength and determination if what was feared becomes real.

Fear of deadly disease, for example, is never easily overcome. Even when conclusive evidence is available that a particular disease cannot be transmitted to others, humans fear proximity because of their innate self-protection mechanisms. Patients with cancer and AIDS know very well how the behaviour of those around them changes when their disease becomes known.

Is it a moral weakness to have fear in cases where logic says it should not exist? Reacting to a powerful base emotion is not morally weak, but avoiding knowledge that could conquer that fear is.

Is it morally wrong to create fear when it is not justified? Those who create fear are usually doing so for their own self-interest to gain money or power. When based on such motives, one must conclude that their actions are not morally correct. There is a fine line between creating fear and pointing out the actual likelihood of some event for which people need to be prepared.

In the computer industry, there is an acronym to describe actions and words that are intended to sow doubt about competitors in the eyes of possible customers. It is called FUD which stands for "Fear, Uncertainty and Doubt". Some company representatives routinely make vague negative suggestions concerning their competitors which cause potential customers and existing clients to pause and think during sales negotiations. Since FUD is a powerful disincentive in the corporate world, merely suggesting it can have a huge effect.

When fear is present, there is only one defence, knowledge. When the unknown becomes known, fear disappears, replaced by action or acceptance.

It is unlikely that fear will ever be eliminated from human existence. But that makes it all the more important that humans constantly strive to learn and push back the boundaries of the unknown.

Of great importance, people must surrender the safety of having faith in what they learned yesterday and learn to accept that the past may not have been perfect or correct. Indeed, the rules by which they have lived may need adjustment from time to time.

But the mere acceptance that the past may have been wrong can create fear in those that regard change with suspicion. It can also create fear in those that worry about their knowledge becoming obsolete. The only advice that can be given is to study change, not reject it out of hand. Change, it is said, is the only constant in life. Therefore, ignoring change is much like closing one's eyes to live in blissful ignorance or hiding one's head in the sand.

Instead of ignoring change or defending the past against it, learn about it and make an objective evaluation. See if it really adds to life. All learning adds to one's knowledge and knowledge is the most powerful weapon against fear.

5) School Years in Chatham

"To strive to be like someone else, regardless of the esteem in which you hold that person, is to lose oneself."

J. F. Sexton

My First Schooling

The first school I attended was just two houses away. It had only been built a few years before I reached the age that I had to attend school but I remember my mother being thankful for the proximity. I do not remember much about my teachers or the lessons, but I do remember getting free milk at morning break. After I was the lucky one to get the bad bottle (the milk came in small refillable glass bottles with cardboard tops), I lost my taste for milk for ever.

I recently found my Grade 1 report card and it is both sad and funny to read. My teacher wrote that she almost wished that I would do something naughty since it just was not normal for a boy to be so attentive and dedicated. In the next term, she wrote that my hospitalization for tonsillitis had seemed to change me and that she feared I was becoming weak. Odd words coming from a teacher. But by the end of the year, I got well above average marks in everything although my mother wrote back that she thought I could do better than the one B that I received, forgetting about the other A's. This started a pattern that I have carried through most of my life, focusing on the small blemishes and ignoring the real accomplishments.

My First Dog

For my 7th birthday, my father surprised me with a new puppy. He was a terrier/beagle mix and I named him Scamp. He and I were always together and I patiently taught him to do many tricks including balancing a treat on his nose and holding it until I said OK. He could hold a cookie on his nose for minutes on end, although everyone could see his obvious anxiety that the treat might somehow disappear. He followed me almost everywhere and even escorted me nightly to bed.

In those days, no one kept dogs on leashes and they roamed the neighbourhood freely. Everyone knew all the local dogs by name. When my neighbours lost a couple of their dogs to traffic, it was a brutal lesson in mortality. Scamp nearly had an abrupt end himself. He came home one evening bloody and in obvious pain. My entire life filled with terror and fear. Dad rushed him to the vet who stitched him up and sent him home the next day. I cannot describe the relief I felt. Dad told me that Scamp's injuries was likely caused by a car, but I always thought the facts did not fit the explanation. I still suspect that he was attacked by a person or persons unknown because he had a puncture wound on his hind leg and a slash across his back. I doubt that a car could do that. I think that my dad wanted to shield me from the possibility that a human being could have deliberately done that to my dog. Sadly though, we all know that some humans can be incredibly cruel to animals.

Perhaps this type of cruel behaviour can be attributed to certain religious teachings that animals are somehow lesser beings than humans since they have no soul or that being reborn as an animal is punishment for life's misdeeds. The simple truth is that all living creatures have a place and a role on our planet and no single species is inherently superior or more valuable than another.

Scamp stayed with me throughout my years in Chatham only to decline in health when I went away to university. Every time I visited home, I could see him growing older and more frail. I knew that the inevitable was near but when I returned home one weekend to hear my father tell me that it was time, I was crushed like I had never been before. I went to my room after hugging Scamp a last time and did not come out until the next day. I will never forget Scamp's eyes that day. They were sad and tired and deep down I knew he just did not enjoy life any more. Even as I write this, the tears have started running down my face. He was the brother I never had, a friend that always kept my most important secrets and someone who was just happy when we were together and wanted nothing more from me than a little play and a kind word.

I have had four dogs since then and every single one of them has had a unique personality and temperament. Except for one of them, they have all been one-of-a-kind, that is they have all been mutts. Fritz, the one that I suspect of being pure-bred, came from an abused background. I did not realize his possible pedigree until a woman who raised bearded collies saw him in the car one day and commented on what a lovely dog he was. Fritz was difficult to befriend because of his mistreatment. Even the vet commented on his shyness with humans. Any loud noise caused him to hide from people. It took two full years of very patient and tender treatment before he finally started to wag his tail with some regularity and show some interest in play. But when I finally achieved that breakthrough, he developed cancer and was lost.

All my dogs have been selected from the lost, abused or cast-offs in the local animal shelters and they have all lived out the remainder of their lives in a loving household. It is a small thing perhaps, but they have all given me great joy and peace despite the dreadful pain I have suffered each time I have lost one. Only fellow animal lovers can really understand this. What they give is something that simply cannot be bought at any price.

Being Singled Out

In Grade 4 my teachers started to recognize my analytical abilities and through a series of tests I was the only one selected from my school to take part in an experimental enhanced learning program. It was being established at another school on the other side of the city. Originally, it was planned to be a four year program from Grades 5 to 8, but ended after Grade 7. The same teacher followed us throughout the three years of the program but subsequently left to begin an academic career at the University of Windsor. I have sometimes pondered if we were an experiment to him or if he honestly hoped to enhance our learning.

I do not recall all of the changes that attending a different school caused, but later in life I remember my mother saying how she had desperately wanted to withdraw me from the program because of how introverted I became. I do remember becoming lost in books rather than play and no longer having any friends in the neighbourhood. Having no siblings against which to measure myself, I did not realize how abnormal my behaviour became for a young boy.

In retrospect, I believe that this enhanced learning program helped me to develop skills in research and critical analysis but failed me when it came to developing personal relationships and an understanding of human behaviour. My life became objective rather than emotive, an imbalance that I only realized much later in life. But it was something that my mother recognized immediately, as any mother would.

Early World Events

I remember quite clearly two events that took place during my early schooling.

The first was the death of Winston Churchill. Everyone in the class was asked to make a scrap book of all the newspaper stories we could find about Churchill and it became, for me, a lesson on both World Wars that was to stay with me for a long time.

The other was the assassination of John Kennedy. I remember we were writing a history test that day and the school janitor tiptoed into the classroom to whisper something to the teacher. After everyone had handed in the test, he announced what had happened. I remember that most folks were emotional and sad, but I was more curious about their reactions because he was the leader of another country, not Canada. I had difficulty understanding why the people around me should be so moved. However, the emotional reaction should not have been a surprise since in Chatham we were dominated by American culture and news. There were only 4 TV channels available (sometimes 5 if the weather and antenna cooperated) and 3 of those were from Detroit.

Puberty

While I was in Grade 7, my body started to change. I was both amazed and embarrassed. Not having an older brother, I really had no idea what was happening. Worse, I was the first of my school mates to experience this and they were both cruel and curious as the changes became obvious during gym period.

I remember vividly in music class having the female teacher stop a song abruptly and demand to know who was deliberately singing off key. When it was my turn to sing solo, she quickly recognized the cracking voice, blushed and excused me from singing for months. I thought it was a punishment and unfair but when friends told me how jealous they were about me not having to sing, it made me feel somewhat better.

Being the subject of much curiosity from my friends opened a window of opportunity for me which was not planned but which I exploited. My first sexual experiences took place with other male friends whose curiosity, rather than sexual orientation, drove their actions. But quickly learning that this type of sex was not socially acceptable kept me from experiencing sex again for many years.

Starting High School

After finishing Grade 8, I was thrust back into the regular school system and had to attend the high school close to home. Once again, I was uprooted from the friends I had made and forced into an environment that was alien to me. I suppose this is something that children of parents who move around the country must experience regularly, but it was uncommon in those days. And without siblings to fall back on, it was difficult.

While my high school was small compared to the other high school in my area of town, it was still immense in my eyes. There were so many kids who I did not know and who existed in closed groups of the same age and background. I eventually found myself gravitating toward others who, like me, seemed to be outside of those groups.

I can see the eyes rolling when I relate how I had to walk to school every day about 1.5 miles in each direction. But in truth, most of other kids either took buses or got rides particularly when the weather turned bad. I cannot say, in retrospect, that this was a bad thing though. It had the benefit of exercise and fresh air and gave me time each day alone with my thoughts. But I could not help feeling jealous of the other kids who had it easier. I suspect all teens are envious or jealous about others they feel have it better than themselves, a theory that is the foundation of most marketing to that age group today.

My walks became exercises in the mathematics of determining how I could save steps. I started to apply my geometry lessons to angles and the distance between points on my way. I actually counted the number of steps taking one angle versus another to prove which way was the shortest. Cutting through a parking lot was good, the best angle to shorten the distance, but I remember being angered by cars parked in my path thereby making my trip longer. I doubt that many teens, then or now, apply geometry and algebra to their trips to and from school.

Learning French

My one sad time academically in high school was my attempt to learn French. In my teenage zeal to learn Canada's other official language, I ran smack into my first real academic wall.

I had visited Montreal during Expo '67 and experienced a certain culture shock when I was unable to understand the people who were standing right next to me in the Metro. Not long afterwards, while I was still in high school, Canada went through the Quebec Crisis and it brought back memories of the disjoint I felt in Montreal. In my naivety, I felt that the only practical thing I could do at that time was to learn French and thereby take one small step to strengthen the country and my sense of being Canadian.

However, the sterile classroom and a complete lack of spoken French in the community made the exercise difficult. But the biggest obstacle was my own brain. I learned later in life that the analytical mind is ill suited to linguistics. Language is not governed by strict rules. It is born of tradition, history and cultural influences. It is the mastery of the exceptions in a language that makes one a true speaker. But my mind struggled to categorize and create rules to remember conjugations, tenses and genders. I could not simply accept what was being said and mimic it like a child learns a language. To my mind that was anarchy, something with which I could not cope.

As a result, French was the only subject that I ever failed in all my school years, including university. My report card actually showed a 50% mark, but I knew that I had failed. I knew because before receiving my marks, the teacher asked me if I was going to take French again and when I said no she replied with obvious relief that I had "just passed". I was crushed and the disappointment has lingered throughout my life. I believe it also had a very practical effect on my psyche later when I tried again to learn the language as an adult.

28

Drugs

My school days in Chatham went from the late 1950's until the early 1970's. These were the days of The Beatles, hippies and revolution. But Chatham was a small city dominated by conservative thinking like so many other small cities around the world.

Nevertheless, I was among the first to grow my hair long and was ridiculed for it. I grew a moustache as soon as I was able which was early in my high school days much to the envy of my friends.

But more than just adopting the outward symbols of the youth revolution that was shaking the world, I was introduced to marijuana, hashish and later to LSD. While alcohol was the drug of choice for most of the guys, I became a regular consumer of acid on the weekends. And I sought out others who were likewise inclined.

While I have never been an advocate of drugs, I do not condemn anyone who has used them. My only concern is with those for whom their drug of choice, whether tobacco, alcohol or other illegal drugs, becomes a necessity in life. Choosing to use a mind or body altering substance is fine. Needing to use one is not.

I found the acid experience to be incredibly liberating. I learned that one should never take things as they appear because there are always complexities hidden from view that one needs to explore if one is to understand life. At the time, I found the whole thing rather mystical and, like most acid users, I regularly thought that I had solved the problems of life during each trip only to forget the solutions the next day.

Sports

In high school, I participated in a number of sports but there are two that stand out in my mind.

First, I was a member of the football team. Having grown early, I was a pretty big kid for my age and so I ended up on the defensive line. Playing games in freezing cold drizzle was no fun, but we advanced all the way to the county championship. I remember my best tackle ever almost like it was yesterday. Our opponents from Wallaceburg had the ball and they tried to run with it around our right side. Throwing my body across the ball carrier's path, he made the cardinal sin of trying to jump over me. Sadly for him, his foot caught my side and he performed an ungraceful flip, landing on his head, knocking him unconscious. Because he was one of their best ball carriers and that tackle kept him out for the rest of the game, it completely shut down their offence and we went on to win the championship.

The other memorable sport in which I participated was track and field. I actually did quite well in the triple jump, despite absolutely no coaching, coming second in the county finals and advancing to the regional competition. Winning there would have meant going to the provincials but I was grossly outclassed at that event. Nevertheless, it was great to have gotten that far.

High School Activities

I was the editor of the high school paper one year and did achieve one thing that had never been done before. Previously, the first edition of the paper had inevitably been the last, but I managed to get out three editions that year and it was duly noted in the yearbook.

I also got very involved with chess which was to become something of a passion for many years. One year, the school sent three of us to the provincial high school championships in Toronto and after a stunning upset start (I managed to hold a draw against one of the tournament favourites in the first round), I quickly faded into an also ran. This was my first nationally rated tournament, and after all was done, I fared the worst of the three of us and started my chess playing career near the bottom of the national rating list.

However, my chess playing continued to improve over time while my athletic career came to a screeching halt after Grade 11.

By the time I left high school, my national chess rating had risen above all my other friends in school and I was close to achieving "expert" level which, in the days before the Spassky-Fischer world championship match in 1972, not many had achieved in this country.

Church

In my early teens I was convinced to join a church group even though I was not really a regular attendee at our local church. In retrospect, I suppose this was some kind of outreach to bring more to the faith. As time moved forward, the group was approached by the minister to conduct a youth-based service for the congregation on a Sunday.

With great enthusiasm, the executive committee of the group agreed and set upon the various tasks that were involved.

What they did not foresee was the need for someone to stand in the pulpit and deliver the sermon. No one wanted to volunteer. Public speaking is difficult for all at first, and difficult for some every time they try. But in this case, since a sermon is meant to deliver an important spiritual message in a manner that is both sincere and convincing, it was a particularly daunting prospect for any young teen. As the search grew desperate for anyone, somehow I managed to be volunteered. I spent hours writing and re-writing my notes worried lest the slightest misspoken word or unintended phrase set the congregation to silent but obvious rage.

However, when the time came, my nerves settled very nicely after the first few words came out of my mouth. This set a precedent for all my later public speaking in front of crowds of varying sizes and temperaments. My nerves would be in overdrive, but the first few words or sentences brought an odd sense of calm and composure which was noted in the audience and relayed back to me with envy by many. By reminding myself sub-consciously that the people sitting out there had come to listen to me and that I actually had something tangible to impart to them, I seldom faced disaster at the lectern.

But my days associated with the church group were numbered. I had not been a regular attendee for many years and there was a certain feeling among the group that I had an obligation to be present if for no other reason than I was now a sort of spokesperson for the group. When my attendance did not change, there were open insults sent my way although not to my face. Therefore, I did the honourable thing under the circumstances and left the group, never to be associated with any religious organization again.

High School Sex

It took me most of high school to come to grips with my sexuality and act upon it. It was clear to me that I had a strong attraction to guys but I knew better than to do anything about it. Even when I was actually approached one day at school, I declined with feigned disdain. Almost everyone, or so it seemed, was having sex except for me.

Finally, after thinking for weeks about it, I decided to approach one of my friends from another school. We often got high on weekends and late one night, when we were alone, I offered myself. After some hesitation, perhaps for the sake of appearances, he consented and I satisfied him. This continued for some time but was never really reciprocated. While that was somewhat frustrating, it was better than nothing and safe from outside knowledge.

In fact, this friend introduced me to a much older man sometime later who had made a pass at him in the city library. That man was attracted to younger men but since, as he explained, I was already a bit old for his tastes, he offered to introduce me to other men in town who would be happy to meet me. These men showed me a very different world, a world for which I had been looking a long time.

Today, I look back on those days with some amusement. It is clear now that these men, deeply in the closet, had formed a tight-knit circle and passed me around like a prize. But at the time, I enjoyed the attention and learned a great deal about our culture and language which was nowhere to be found in books and was passed down strictly as oral history. It was an opening to a world about which I had dreamt and was now experiencing.

Other Hobbies

I had only two real hobbies during these years, reading and building models. I never really caught on to car models, but I loved aeroplanes, ships and armoured vehicles.

I read voraciously, spending most of my allowance on weekly trips to the book store. During Canada's centennial year, I set out to read a minimum of 100 pages a day for the entire year. I am not only proud to say that I accomplished my goal, but I am also proud to say that most of the books I read were non-fiction which was rather unusual for a boy of 14 going on 15. I have never lost the habit of reading, but I have to say that I do not do as much of it these days. That habit has been somewhat transformed by the new mediums of communication. I now have access to documents from across the world through the magic of the Internet. It still amazes me that I can read things from places that I will likely never visit and from perspectives that I never knew even existed 50 years ago. I can satisfy any whimsical curiosity that arises within seconds. It is truly astonishing and intellectually gratifying.

I spent most of what was left of my allowance on plastic models. But after building so many of them, I did not feel the same sense of accomplishment as when I began. So I found something rather unusual in North American modelling, paper models printed in Germany. Learning a few basic words in German, I cut, folded and glued endless tiny pieces of paper to make a few warships. My best effort was a First World War pre-dreadnought. It took perhaps more than 500 hours to finish but it still sits in a glass case my father built for it. He was amazed at my persistence to see it to the end. The gun turrets swivel, the gun barrels elevate and the cranes turn. I could never do such a thing again because of worsening sight and hands that grow more clumsy with age. I finally gave up a year or so after starting this type of modelling when an aircraft carrier I was assembling required more than a dozen aircraft to be built for the flight deck. I finished a grand total of one plane. It had almost 90 pieces and was just an inch and a half long. I simply could not bear the thought of doing another eleven of those planes.

World Events During High School

My high school years were dominated by Vietnam, hydrogen bomb testing, the cold war, and racial riots in the USA. All of these things had an effect on me and the way I think, and those effects have lingered with me since.

I witnessed the lies being propagated by governments to support their exercise of power, particularly during the Vietnam war. The press was, I believe, more free in those days to report the reality of life and death in both war and civil unrest. It was ugly, not clean and surgical as depicted today. The reality is that all armed conflicts are ugly, at least to those who suffer during them. And those who have suffered often become bitter and angry and potential future enemies based on their desire for revenge. Regardless of how "just" a war may be portrayed, to those who have lost family, friends and property it is unjustifiably brutal and evil. The cleanliness of battle pictures from 5,000 feet in the air is a god-send for the spin doctors but those pictures should not make us forget that people are dying as those bombs explode.

The two most important events during those years that have stayed with me were the Quebec Crisis, which I did not quite understand at the time, and the landing of a man on the moon.

My understanding of the Quebec Crisis was mostly concerned with the removal of Canadians' civil rights by the invocation of the War Measures Act. While nothing untoward happened in my part of the country, it meant great anxiety and lingering hard feelings in Quebec. I was simply unaware of the fundamental causes of the crisis and focused solely on the consequences. I have since grown to understand, as well as anyone outside that environment can, the discontent generated by the mistreatment of francophone Quebecers.

The reality of that discontent is shared by a number of groups that I have since been privy to know and with whom I even have some affinity. One of my best friends in later life was a Mohawk elder with whom I shared much time and fun. I witnessed many times how he was viewed and treated in society as different, not equal. In earlier days, I hung around with a Chinese-Canadian friend who, on one occasion, was openly insulted with racial slurs at a corner store. When I travelled with a wonderfully humorous Jamaican-Canadian woman for business, I noticed the odd looks when the two of us went out for dinner.

Canada has done better in many respects than the United States in terms of tolerance and acceptance of racial and cultural differences. An African-American friend who was visiting told me how he was surprised at the number of people who, being ahead of him, would open a door and then invite him to go ahead. He told me that was rare in America and that he was very impressed with this country and its people. But despite his observations, Canadians still have a long way to go.

I have to say that my views have matured regarding francophone Quebec today. While I greatly appreciate Canada as my birth country, I have seen many civil wars around the globe caused by the frustrations of a people who feel a certain disconnect with the rest of the country's citizens. The FLQ crisis brought Canada closer to conflict than at any other time since the Riel Rebellion. But I believe there are fundamental questions to ask when one's neighbours are unhappy with the *status quo*. Is that *status quo* worth the ultimate defence, war? Since I believe that all war is irrational, then other solutions need to be sought.

In response to the ongoing challenge of Quebec nationalism, the Canadian federal government passed the Clarity Act. It gave the federal government the right to ignore any referendum on independence if it disagreed with the question on the ballot. But that displays an arrogant attitude because it seeks to veto the public will through the guise of protecting them from being duped. On the other side, Quebec sovereignists continue to demand that Quebec must be defined by its current borders. Those borders were decided long ago without regard to the linguistic and ethnic heritage of the resident populations and it is therefore wrong to use those borders to define a francophone nation.

Regardless of the question put, as long as there are contiguous areas with a relatively homogeneous francophone culture that have enough population to sustain a modern country and whose population votes to form their own national government, then they should have the right to do so. While drawing borders under these conditions would be tough, it would be a fundamentally better solution and avoid the horrible mistakes made by most colonial governments who drew lines on maps without regard to tribe or culture in Africa and many other areas. Is there any good reason to force someone to live in a place and under a government where they do not feel at home? This is a classic case of people becoming lost in passion and rhetoric and thus failing to find good solutions.

The other profound event, the landing on the moon, was a magical moment for me. Of all the changes and events that have taken place in my lifetime, I think this was the most significant for me, at least to date. This was true history happening before my eyes. There is no doubt in my mind that this event will forever be remembered by humanity and is far more important than, say, the first Europeans to traverse the Atlantic. It ought to be remembered that those sailors, as brave as they were, discovered nothing that other humans did not know and call home already.

My single greatest regret looking forward is that I will never be able to leave this planet and look back at it like those pioneers. Age will prevail before such travel becomes common place. To travel even further and witness the marvels of Mars or the moons of Jupiter is almost beyond my dreams. This century's tourists will make such voyages and I can only envision that possibility with the twin sins of envy and jealousy. But for the sake of all, I hope that the tourists of the future will not pollute these exotic places with souvenirs of their visits, thus keeping the cosmos a pristine marvel for all time. Contrary to popular belief, we were not given domain over the universe to do with it what we please. We are guests in this place and we should behave as such because our stay will eventually end.

The accomplishment of going to the moon was the culmination of many minds developing both the theories and the tools required to make the voyage. Then again, what great thing has not been the result of many minds and hands. Throughout my own career, I cannot think of one idea of mine that was truly original. I stood on the knowledge and insight of many to construct something that was different from the experience of the folks around me. But it was merely algebra to add two or more ideas together and come up with something that others may have missed.

On that summer evening in 1969, the moon landing was truly a once in a lifetime experience and a giant step for humanity. I sat in the living room, transformed as I watched and listened to an actual person stepping onto another celestial body. After that, I have always felt that to use the expression, "once in a lifetime", for any lesser event demeans the phrase and the accomplishment.

6) Life and the Universe

"It is important to constantly challenge one's own opinions and beliefs. As new facts are discovered and deeper understandings evolve, a failure to re-evaluate one's own self is a failure to grow and become a better person."

J. F. Sexton

Cause and effect. Presumably one begets the other, but which comes first. Is an event the effect of some cause or is it the cause of some effect. Events that cause some effect must have been themselves the result of some cause. In this sense, everything becomes relative to the perspective with which it is viewed.

Humans put a certain perspective on everything they examine, including themselves. The human perspective on life is determined by that which is observable. Since there appears to be a beginning and an end to all living things, humans find it easy to believe in a beginning and an end to absolutely everything they observe.

The infinite is so removed from human experience and understanding that it becomes something beyond their capability to really appreciate and fathom. At best, peoples' minds cope with their known ancestors and their hoped progeny. Sometimes, that is expanded by visiting things that were built, like the pyramids, or born, like dinosaurs, in the distant past which reinforces the notion of how brief the existence of an individual really is.

It should not be a surprise then, that the very notion of a beginning and an end to life has become the bedrock assumption of human investigation of the universe.

But it is common knowledge that assumptions can be risky.

Generally accepted scientific theory today agrees with virtually every religious teaching, saying that there was a starting point to the universe. Religions talk about creation. Science talks about the "big bang".

Scientists continue to look for evidence of the singularity

which they believe was the universe's starting point. When they observe things that match the theoretical model, they feel great satisfaction. When they observe things that contradict the model, they seek new ways to explain the contradiction within the accepted framework. Thus, when their understanding of the laws of physics was insufficient to explain the first micro-seconds of existence, the theory of inflation was constructed to get around the problem. The theory of inflation deemed that the laws of physics did not apply during that very first moment of existence. Conveniently, this also allows for the creation and beginning of the laws of physics at a later point in time. It begins to echo the six days of creation in the Holy Bible, and all the other myths in the distant past about how humanity arrived at this place.

Every great leap forward in humanity's understanding of the universe has come when some individual eventually puts all the contradictions into an entirely new model that makes the previously accepted model appear archaic and even primitive. It is the same for every human endeavour. It is the brave soul that steps back and concludes that current theory cannot be correct and does something about it, often at great expense to professional career and reputation.

Looking at another example, it is generally accepted that the universe is expanding from its beginning at the big bang, and that the distance between each galaxy is increasing. Yet, it is observable that our nearest large galaxy, Andromeda, is on a collision course with the Milky Way. It is also observable that galaxies have collided in the distant past. Today, it is explained that it is actually galaxy clusters that are moving apart, not galaxies. Galaxies appear to contain enough mass for gravity to hold them together and even draw some of them closer to each other, thereby overcoming the inertial force of the big bang.

To explain why gravity is too weak at that distance to draw galaxy clusters together, some additional force had to be boosting the inertial momentum created by the big bang. This mysterious new force has been called dark energy and is used to explain the expanding universe and the expansion of space itself. There is an active scientific debate concerning which force is greater, gravity or dark energy. If gravity is stronger than dark energy then the universe will reach a maximum size and then begin to contract, like an elastic snapping back, presumably to the singularity from which it sprung. If dark energy is stronger than gravity then the universe will continue to expand until all the energy in the stars is exhausted and everything freezes to nearly absolute zero. In either case, that will be the end of the universe.

But the theory of the big bang and the multiple theories concerning the end of the universe are all based on the assumption that there must have been a beginning to everything and there will be an end.

That basic assumption may indeed be proved correct, but on the other hand it may not. No less a scientist than Einstein believed that there was no beginning and there would be no end to the universe.

To grasp the infinite requires an exceptional mind. To have had a beginning begs the question about time before that. To have an end begs the question about what is next. It is all in the perspective with which things are viewed. Cause and effect, if you will.

Humans assume that life had a beginning on this planet. There would seem to be some logic in that assumption since the planet appears to be a little over 4 billion years old and thus life could not have existed on it before the planet's own beginning. The oldest evidence of living things on this planet dates to just over 3 billion years ago. But it is not known if life began here or if it was seeded here from organic matter scattered throughout the universe.

Some attribute the cause of life's origins on this planet to a supernatural being and some to a biochemical evolutionary process. At least there is one shared idea between the two which is the common thread of a beginning.

With the exception of Hindus and Buddhists, who believe in an endless cycle of rebirth, most humans also assume an end to life on this planet. They believe the end will come as some form of punishment or Armageddon from a god or gods, or they study the death of the sun or some other human-made catastrophe. In all those scenarios, life ends.

Humans make other assumptions about life. For example, they regularly attribute hierarchical values to life forms. From the earliest historical recordings, humans have assumed preeminence over all other species, first based on some divine gift, then based on their superior dexterity and intelligence. For every other species, humans attribute value based on the uses to which they can put it. In history, some humans even put a value on other humans based on the use to which they could put them.

Today, humans put every other living thing into categories, treating some as valuable, others as pests. Since very few societies have given the "right to life" to other species (as they have to themselves), humans routinely try to destroy those species which they see as hindering their progress and preserve those that they see as having value.

In their arrogance, humans assumed early in history that they were alone in the universe, created uniquely by the gods. Thus they were given domain over their surroundings to do with as they pleased.

However, scientists have started recently to seek out life elsewhere in the universe based on the massive odds in favour of such a proposition. It is difficult to imagine the consequences of discovering even bacteria elsewhere in the universe. Will it shake the bedrock belief that humanity was divinely created and given dominion over the universe or will religion develop new interpretations?

In reality, the discovery of bacteria may not be enough to alter ancient beliefs, but scientists are really hoping to find life that is similar to life on this planet. They search for Earth-like planets in the so-called habitable zone around distant stars to improve the odds of success. They listen through radio telescopes for signs of civilizations that have evolved communication abilities similar to ours.

It is important to pause for a moment to think about this proposition. Regardless of how and when life began on this planet, it has evolved to its current forms based on the changing environment, other competing life forms and even singular events, like the impact of asteroids. Life on the planet today bears little resemblance to life on the planet even 100 million years ago. Therefore, it is unlikely that humans will ever find other human-like beings on other planets. Life will be found, but it will be very different from *homo sapiens*.

Will intelligent life be found?

First, what is "intelligent" life? Can intelligence be defined only by the ability to leave a record of events? Or is intelligence better defined by behaviour, that is the ability to react differently to exactly the same stimuli and conditions. Not having a very good definition of "intelligent life", could there have been intelligent life forms in the distant past on this planet that did not leave any evidence of their existence simply because they did not have the dexterity to do so? Mental abilities are not the same as physical abilities.

Humans now search for life and, more importantly, intelligent life on other planets in the universe. But the fundamental problem is that the search is narrowly focused on finding another planet with similar conditions and history to that of Earth, when in fact, life may have evolved in wondrous ways in environments that are deadly to the kind of life known here. It is also distinctly possible that life elsewhere may not have evolved to communicate in the manner scientists expect and for which they search.

Nature continues to surprise every day with its ability to do things that humans thought impossible only yesterday. Humans continue to find extremophile species living on Earth in environments previously thought to be completely hostile to life. Life exists in the ice of Antarctica. It exists miles beneath the surface of the ocean, absent any sunlight, living off the minerals and energy coming from thermal vents. It exists in lakes of extreme alkalinity that would burn the hands.

In this solar system, it turns out that the Earth's moon has water and that both Jupiter and Saturn have their own system of orbital bodies that are as diverse and astonishing as anything the great science fiction writers of the past could imagine. There is a moon which appears to have a giant salt-water ocean beneath its ice. There is a moon that has lakes formed from rain made of liquid methane. Discoveries continue almost daily that would have been considered outrageous had they been predicted fifty years ago.

Nevertheless, scientists' definition of life is narrowly determined by their innate bias of what they think life must be. There may be value in searching for life that is similar to what is found on Earth, but only to the extent that it may simplify communication with, and understanding of, that life.

But scientists must be alert to life that defies their preconceived notions, particularly intelligent life. For example, some jellyfish on Earth have been found to have a kind of decision-making process to pursue prey despite the fact they lack brains. Humans do not yet know how that works. In fact, intelligence may exist in life forms that cannot be expressed through the types of communication humans commonly expect. Would a human who is unable to speak or write be considered less intelligent than other humans? Similarly would any creature with decision-making capabilities and memory be considered lacking intelligence simply because it lacked opposing thumbs to write and build things?

All matter has both a common ancestry and a common composition created by the awesome power of the stars and the brilliant simplicity of their workings. It is just gravity working on matter to create heat, thereby fusing atoms and creating new elements. In fact, all of nature works with elegant simplicity. Nature just scales things up to unimaginable proportions to confuse and confound our senses.

It is simply arrogant for humans to feel any sense of superiority in this universe. It may come to be understood that humanity is unique but only because no other species in the universe has evolved in an environment and a history like Earth. Being unique, however, does not mean being more important or deserving, something humans should never forget.

A god or gods did not create the universe but the universe ought still to inspire humility and reverence for its breathtaking vastness and power. After all, this planet and all that live upon it are its creations.

All life is precious regardless of when and how it was created. The cause of life on this planet may never come to be fully understood, but the effect of that life can be seen all around. Life here does not always peacefully coexist but only one species on this planet has shown the tendency to destroy all around it in what it perceives as its own self-interest. That species is the parasite *homo sapiens*.

Humans have an obligation not to squander the resources of this planet. The odds would appear to suggest that the Earth is indeed unique simply because of its evolutionary history as a satellite of the Sun. It is not enough to live by the motto "because we can" to ravage the planet. Scientists continue to see signs that other life forms on this planet have intelligence and it ought to be with shame that humanity continues to drive many of those species to extinction.

Humanity must move beyond its human-centric thinking and grow in its understanding of the world and universe around it. It is only then that *homo sapiens* will mature as a species. Perhaps the discovery of life beyond its current comprehension will indeed wake humanity to its humble place in the universe.

7) *School Years Away From Home*

> *"Research enlightens the world, except when it is based on false assumptions."*
>
> *J. F. Sexton*

Beginning University

I left home in 1971 to attend university in Waterloo, not at the University of Waterloo, but at Waterloo Lutheran University. It was the last private university in Ontario but that was to end when the province took it over mid-way through my undergraduate years. In an effort to keep much of the memorabilia of the university relevant, the province was convinced to rename it Wilfrid Laurier University thereby keeping the initials and it was under that name that I graduated with an Honours B.A. In 1975.

The only real reason I choose WLU was because of a small bursary they gave me for my high school grades. I guess I should have learned then and there that money talks, because for the grand sum of $200 I was lured away from Western and the University of Toronto.

But it was not a bad choice in the grand scheme of things as it turned out. Classes were small, not just for fourth year students but even for many first year students. I got to know many of the professors and glimpsed at some of their life stories through bits and pieces of anecdotes.

One of them talked of being under a death sentence in the USSR. He was an Estonian exile who left at the end of World War II. I recently read about his work in Estonia during its brief independence from the Soviet Union prior to the Second World War, his work to document Estonian culture while here in Canada and, sadly, his passing in 1995. He had a wonderful old world dignity and manners that are seldom seen today. I remember vividly sitting in his office when we both reached for a cigarette at the same time. Without thinking, we simultaneously offered each other a smoke and, after a small pause, we each accepted the other's offer. I liked that man both for the ideals to which he had literally committed his life and for his understated wisdom. I regret not really internalizing that from him until much later in life.

My first year went well, except for my course on philosophy. You may well wonder about my qualifications to write this book on my own philosophical ideas when I just barely passed a course studying the great philosophers of the past. But there is a difference between studying those that went before and trying to escape from the burden of the past to see things in a fresh critical way. It is said that to forget the past dooms one to repeat its mistakes. I do not forget those great thinkers of history, but they were all trying to see and explain things in ways that were not the common understanding of things in their time. In a very modest way, that is also what I am trying to do.

But I digress.

I mentioned smoking which was a habit I picked up only when I started university. Perhaps it was pressure from my peers or just the pressure of school, but my habit quickly grew into major proportions. Only when I travelled home did I resist the urge to smoke. Although both my parents smoked, I was just too embarrassed to smoke in front of them for several years.

Enduring all my youth in a smoking household shaped my tolerance and even sympathy for smokers today. Despite quitting cold turkey from a three-pack-a-day habit in the mid-eighties, I have never minded smokers around me and even now keep ashtrays in my home.

Many of my undergraduate days were spent nursing hangovers. I vividly remember the horrible schedule I had on Mondays during my fourth year. I had 10 hours of classes that day and only five hours during the rest of the week. A group of us with similar Mondays would gather after all of our classes were finished that day and drink ourselves into unconsciousness by closing time.

In my summer holidays during those years, I had a couple of jobs but the best, meaning highest paying, was in an auto-parts factory. Being high paying was the sole positive attribute about that job. The plant operated 24 hours a day, employing three shifts and everyone, except a privileged few, changed shifts every two weeks from days to nights to evenings going counter-clockwise so to speak. I remember the brutal affects of adjusting my body to ever changing schedules. Trying to sleep in south-western Ontario during the heat of the day when temperatures soared to 90°F or more and the humidity lingered in the 80 to 90 percent range, is something I will never regret leaving.

There is nothing particularly bad about factory work *per se*, but working an assembly line can quickly dehumanize a person who does not look after their mental well being. In those days, before much of the automation and robotics we see today, humans became part of the line working to the machine's rhythm and speed. I quickly learned to challenge my brain to complex arithmetic calculations while my body simply reacted like an automaton keeping time to the rhythm of the assembly line. I have no idea if I correctly solved the problems I posed to myself since they involved dividing four digit numbers into eight digit numbers, but the mental exercise took me away from the monotony and kept me sane.

The one fantastic consolation from those days was membership in the United Auto Workers. The UAW is the only union that I ever joined, mostly because it was mandatory for employment at that factory. But the union card allowed me to take my friends to the UAW union hall for cheap beer during the school year. It was a ticket to popularity. I never joined the Public Service Alliance of Canada (PSAC) or the Professional Institute of the Public Service (PIPS) despite being eligible simply because I never felt there was much benefit in doing so. When the government is the employer, it has the legislative power to set pay and conditions regardless of the collective bargaining process and has done so on many occasions. Under those circumstances, unions have only the power to embarrass governments but with little public sympathy for civil servants even that power has very limited use.

But now for a quick reality check. In those days a glass of draft beer could be bought for as little as $0.20. That is right, just twenty cents. Then again the average salary was under $10,000. It was only during the days of hyper-inflation in the late Seventies and early Eighties that salaries began to shoot up to modern levels.

My four years at Wilfrid Laurier passed quickly. I majored in political science and was drawn with some fascination to examine the other side of the cold war as it existed in those days. My chess playing from high school had become something of an obsession. I even authored a column in the university's bi-weekly student newspaper about chess. Since most of the best players in the world lived behind the Iron Curtain, that was perhaps my inspiration for studying the Soviet block. But I do not consciously recall making that choice, I just went with my feelings.

In fact, I can say now, in retrospect, that most of my life has been intuitive rather than planned. Planning my own future was never my forte. Planning major projects and group efforts was easy for me. But until much later in life, I just allowed other people to plan my own future.

My chess playing did result in one unusual opportunity while I was in Waterloo. A professor of psychology at the University of Waterloo was doing a study on short-term memory using chess players as his subjects. He invited me first to be a guinea pig and then to liaise with the chess playing community locally to obtain other subjects. His study found a high correlation between a player's national rating and that player's short-term memory capacity. I did not find anything surprising in that result. But my own result was way off the expected curve, being much higher than it ought to have been based on my national rating. The professor removed my scores from his study on the basis that I was assisting in the study and once they were removed his charts looked much more consistent with his hypothesis. However my own test scores encouraged me to think that I could do much better at the game than my current rating suggested and I eventually proved that to be the case.

During those years, everyone expected things from me, but I just enjoyed doing the things that brought me feelings of accomplishment. In high school, they expected me to become a scientist because of my abilities in logic and mathematics, but I wanted to teach and enjoyed history. In university, I did well in courses that required precision, but enjoyed more the courses that were grey despite not doing as well in them. My thought processes never quite seemed to match those of my professors since I often challenged orthodoxy. I believe it was my inability to fully articulate my thoughts that frustrated my professors more so than the non-orthodox thoughts themselves.

My Sexual Re-awakening

During my time at WLU, I finally started to push myself to meet other people who shared my sexual desires.

In 1969, the Stonewall Riots took place when the gays of New York City revolted against oppressive police harassment. Like the civil rights movement before it, the gay rights movement took hold and spread across the continent and even to Europe. Those events seemed far away to me, but then I started to see some people who recognized that gays were not inherently wicked to be punished simply for being who they were. While the majority of these early acceptors were women, there was a scattering of men as well.

Still, I did not feel comfortable going to gay bars and made efforts not to be seen when I did get the courage to go. Looking back, it was a horrible time when the majority of men would have had no hesitation to teach a fag a lesson. But it was a relief to meet a few local men and have some fun with my own kind. It should be remembered that there were no Gay Pride events in those days. Virtually everyone was in the closet, so to speak.

I finally went to a meeting of gays at the university, held in a room that was rather difficult to find at first. There I met my first love, a love which lasted only a short time and resulted in a difficult break-up. Like everything else in my life, though, I learned something from that experience and I never made the same mistakes again.

Moving to Ottawa

In 1975, I moved to the nation's capital, Ottawa. It was a smaller place then, definitely known for rolling up the sidewalks after 6:00pm. But it was the nation's capital and the centre of political life.

I had intended to take a Master's degree in political science at Carleton University but after I read more in the school's calendar I ended up applying to the School of Soviet and Eastern European Studies unaware that it was a separate degree program. Once again, I found myself at the mercy of fate rather than my brain.

As things turned out, though, it was a good choice since the program had only a few graduate students and felt very much like the smaller more intimate environment I had left at WLU. In fact, a number of the students in the program were military types who were trying to advance their careers through learning more about our cold war opponents. I found it intriguing to be among people who already had careers and were clearly more serious about the program than others, including myself.

Because there were few of us and we lacked the competitive need to outshine each other for job opportunities like the engineering students, we formed a very close knit friendly group. We studied and socialized extensively together. On many a weekend evening, we would gather to play penny-ante poker and share a few beers. While I certainly did not win enough to pay my tuition, I do remember one special evening when things could not go wrong for me. I began winning a couple of hands and then got bolder as I won again and again. When I finally lost my first hand, I had racked up 26 winning hands in a row. It was just one of those nights of luck when my bluffs were not called and, when the other guys did call, I had the better hand. Since that night, nothing like that has ever repeated itself for me.

Because of the move to Ottawa, I was able to get more serious about my chess playing. Ottawa was a much larger place than Waterloo and there were many good players resident in the capital. Gradually, I improved my national rating and reached the "expert" level which is one level below master. I played during the week at a local club and in a number of weekend tournaments in the region. One year, I even lead the Carleton University team when it competed in the North American University Team Championships held in Columbus, Ohio. We did not fare very well, but did not embarrass ourselves either.

The year 1976 was the American bi-centennial and the United States Chess Federation (USCF) proposed a match with Canada to take place along the full length of the border. I was fortunate enough to be selected as part of the team from Eastern Ontario that played the Americans in Brockville. Teams at many border crossings played that day and while Canada lost, we did not lose by much. All players received a commemorative medal from the USCF which I still have hanging on my trophy shelf.

My course work progressed reasonably well but the real task

was to complete a thesis at the end of the program. I believe the most difficult thing for most graduate students is the selection of a thesis topic. Few students find it a simple task unless they have been focused on one particular topic for some time. Most students struggle to find something that can capture and keep their interest through the significant time it takes to research and write a thesis. I selected an initial topic and started research work on it but just did not find anything that inspired me. Then, a different idea came to me and I proceeded to dig into it with some vigour.

I had seen a lot of work done on the Soviet system of youth socialization, but virtually all of it was focused on the Komsomol which was for older youths. Very little had been written on the associations for younger children, namely the Little Octobrists and the Young Pioneers. If nothing else, it gave me a very open field to examine. These youth groups were for children in the earliest grades to high school. If you have seen the sort of demonstrations put on in North Korea by very young children all dressed alike, then you have some idea of the type of organizations these were.

Since there was virtually nothing written about these groups in English, most of my work focused on translating Russian-language books and pamphlets published in the USSR. It was very labour intensive, often with little meaningful material found. Publications in the USSR at that time were heavily monitored and filled with positive propaganda pictures. Piercing the rosy veil was difficult.

I did not set out with any particular conclusion in mind, but a picture started to form of the discrepancy between the rosy description of the youth groups and the reality of Soviet life with shortages and corruption. It seemed to me that such a gap which could not be concealed must lead to questions that could not easily be answered by the children themselves.

So I built my thesis around the idea that the gap between the world portrayed to these very young children and the reality of daily life was certain to cause inner conflict, and would likely result in political disaffection as those children grew up. Even if the family unit was staunchly in support of the system, the credibility gap between the lessons learned in school and the harshness of life had to create doubts in the minds of the children.

Indeed, within 20 years of that conclusion, with the introduction of *glasnost* and *perestroika* which publicly admitted that gap, the Soviet bloc collapsed with such quickness that the entire world was taken aback. I cannot say, with all due honesty, that I predicted that outcome but the collapse did seem to me to be the result of the disaffection which I had suggested was taking place.

When I presented my thesis, I was pleased by the comment of one of the readers who said that I had almost convinced him of the success of the Soviet socialization program until I then showed how it could not work in the long term. Being able to see the other perspective and accurately understanding it was becoming one of my strengths, and that strength has benefited me greatly ever since.

In 1978, I was finally awarded a Master's degree in "Soviet and East European Studies", having just missed the deadline for graduation the previous year. When I was actually handed the degree, I had already started down another accidental path in my life, a path that was to be my life's career.

Before leaving the subject of my Master's degree, I should add that while it would seem to have been a rather wasteful exercise to obtain it, I did gain a considerable amount from the course. Obviously, those gains were not in the sense of being able to apply the specific knowledge gained to my future career. But I gained in other ways.

As an adult, I have always felt that education has three primary purposes, to build one's knowledge base, to hone one's research abilities and to sharpen one's sense of logic and scepticism. My graduate degree met and exceeded the last two criteria and has served me well throughout my life. As for the knowledge base, I did stash away a bunch of information, most of which is now history rather than current politics, but I have had a number of occasions to trot out one factoid or another from those days. Storing away bits of information, no matter how obscure or seemingly irrelevant, is never a waste of time. I have need from time to time of my high school chemistry, mathematics and biology despite being sure, at the time, that those subjects would never help me in later life.

8) Male Sex and Sexuality

"Morality is not normal. Morality is humanity's way of putting limits on its own natural behaviour to make it appear that it is above its animal roots. But in trying to be above those roots, humanity has taken up other evils, such as war and religion, to enforce one morality over another."

J. F. Sexton

It is difficult for most men to imagine and discuss female sexuality since it is completely outside of their experience. Men are neither women nor do they spend many hours in deep discussion with women about their sexuality.

Professionals also have difficulty separating socialized behaviour from instinct and hormone driven lust.

But from observing men and being subject to the same biological and social forces that shape men, it is safe to say that men are deeply driven by their sexuality and sexual urges. In public, most men try very hard to rise above those urges which they rationalize as base and animalistic. They strive to be "civilized" by denying the physical needs created by their hormones.

In the male dominated ruling classes of earlier times, men found it necessary and mutually advantageous to make laws governing their sexual behaviour. To protect their property, which wives were considered, they made laws against sexual relations outside of marriage. In many ways, marriage was really an ownership contract blessed by religious authorities. It is only in the last 100 years or so that women have begun to escape from these restrictive and discriminatory laws to become "persons" before the law with all the rights that status provides.

But men still cling to a set of rules to ensure that there are boundaries limiting what they might otherwise do. Men who violate the marital sanctity of another, or carry away another man's daughter, can expect legal or physical retribution. Men also punish women for straying, or appearing to stray, from their relationship. This may seem a carryover from the days when women were property, but there is likely more to it than that.

The basis of most rules governing adult sexual behaviour does not flow purely from some moralistic philosophy, but seem to flow from an ancient unspoken sexual contract among men that a woman, once spoken for, was off limits to other men. Women not yet attached could only be approached with the permission of their fathers. By this unspoken contract, men guarded their sexual outlets against all other potential rivals. Clearly, this was mutually beneficial for most men. There was even an unspoken understanding that the breaking of this sacred contract was a legitimate pretence to commit violence. While these notions flow from very ancient times, they are deeply ingrained within the male psyche.

This behaviour is not much different from the behaviour of many species of mammals in which males attempt to gather as many females as possible for their own benefit and will fiercely defend their harems against all other males. Since male animals who have acquired one or more sexual partners cannot take advantage of a legal system, they resort to tooth and claw to defend their sexual outlets.

While death is infrequently a result of harem poaching in the animal kingdom, human males often have easy access to weapons which can lead to the death of the poacher and/or the death of the female who sought escape from the relationship. It is more common, however, to see vitriolic divorce battles. Even for the unmarried, there are frequent brawls in bars between two men over some potential female sexual partner.

Are human males really that far removed from their animal instincts?

Most men conform to the contract both socially and at work and so the incidents of violence as a result of breaking the contract are relatively low. In many ways, men even push each other to higher levels of conformity with ever tighter restrictions. In the modern workplace, for example, where women are present in ever larger numbers, any activity which might inflame the male libido has been forbidden by both policy and law. It has become increasingly rare to see liaisons, which can grow into sexual partnerships, within the workplace because of the fear of harassment charges. In addition, the naughty jokes and provocative images have all become off limits.

However, the male sex drive is such that it constantly pushes men to seek sexual outlets wherever and whenever they can be found. Men will risk the consequences of breaking the sexual contract if they believe they can escape detection. The examples of this are so numerous that it becomes the norm rather than the exception. How often does the public witness politicians, who have much to lose, being exposed for some sexual exploit. Within groups of their own sex, men will often joke about such things but the jokes are thinly veiled expressions of pride by the teller and envy or jealousy from the listeners. In mixed company, the very same men will express outrage and disgust with respect to the incident that was the subject of their jokes only a short time ago.

Outside of the work place, where there is greater possibility to escape detection, all men stay alert for possibilities. Some even court those possibilities by finding reason and time to frequent areas known for the presence of both female and male professionals who understand the perpetual demand. There is good reason why the "world's oldest profession" continues to flourish despite public expressions of moral indignation.

Every man caught or confronted in such a situation will attempt to deny the obvious or confess weakness. They seek to avoid the consequences of breaking that deeply internalized contract. But despite being caught, they will still pursue sex if the opportunity presents itself, albeit with more discretion, and other men will secretly admire their success.

Men who are committed to the contract and who do not wish to break it, still require a sexual outlet. It is for that reason the pornography industry flourishes for men. Perhaps it says something about their sex drives that women have not fostered a similarly successful industry for themselves. Through porn, men can give their fantasies free rein and let their minds go to places they dare not go in real life. Surely, it should come as no surprise that the porn industry grosses billions in the Western world despite being the unending target of the moral police. It fills a very deep need and is the only practical alternative to acting upon those urges with another person.

However, there is a group of men for whom the sexual contract described above does not exist or is weak at best. They have no need to protect their female sexual outlets from other men. They know that they are not treading on another man's turf when they have sex. They are men who seek out other men for sex.

This group of men allows their biological drive free rein when they are safely within an environment of similar men. It is not uncommon, therefore, for these men to have hundreds, even thousands, of sexual partners during their lives. There is no guilt or shame in this behaviour except that which is imposed by others.

But describing it in this way would seem to imply that these men make a choice to have sex with other men. That is not true. No less than Nobel prize winner, Bishop Desmond Tutu, remarked how incredible it would be to think that men would freely choose to have sex with other men knowing the social consequences of their actions.

Only men who have satisfying relations with both females and other males seem to be capable of making a choice. They seem to be able to achieve satisfaction based on convenience and opportunity. But men who seek out other men exclusively do not do so out of conscious choice, they do so out of some undetermined biological drive.

In many societies and throughout most of the history of civilization, men who sought out other men as sexual partners have been persecuted, even to death. Why is that? Most would argue that it is a result of religious dogma, based on the need to propagate the species.

But might that antipathy be based on jealousy or fear? Could jealousy be generated when men who are constrained by their own sexual contract see the sexual freedom enjoyed by men who seek other men. Or could it be simply that men committed to the contract fear the very presence of unmarried adult males who they presume might be poachers. If human males truly have an inherited mammalian instinct to block any possible poacher, then it would make "civilized" sense to force all adult males into their own contract. By lowering the number of single adult males in society, the odds of every male keeping their sexual outlet to themselves are improved.

Indeed, while it is absurd to believe that there is any real threat to male-female partnerships, it is likely that forcing all men to marry guaranteed their commitment to the contract and removed suspicion. Thus, enacting laws against homosexual behaviour was a powerful tool to drive all men into the fold.

Based on the overwhelming social pressure by other men to marry, men who have sex with men frequently experience fear of how other men will perceive them. They fear, first, being perceived as a threat to lure away female partners and, second, having an abundance of riches among those who have little. Guilt through abundance has also driven some of these men to turn to the heterosexual model of a formal marriage contract as a means to blend into the majority. It is very much like forgoing the outward signs of wealth in an effort not to antagonize the poor.

But there is a fundamental contradiction between the free expression of the sex drive in men who are attracted to men and the self-imposed restraints of a sexual contract by marriage. What is to be gained by such a contract for men who seek out other men? Forgoing an abundance of sex in an effort to achieve equal social standing based on the heterosexual model of family and sexual restraint seems a high price to pay. It is not only a high price but raises fierce antagonism in many of those for whom these acts are meant to demonstrate "normal" social behaviour.

In fact, there is little to suggest to opponents of gay marriage that this is "normal" compared to their concept of that state. At best, it starts to generate acceptance of different social models, breaking down previously accepted notions of normalcy. At worst, it is seen as a mockery of the limitations of their sexual contract and engenders deeper resentment.

In the end, though, all men will continue to be driven by their biological urges. No matter how civilized humans become, they cannot escape their animal roots regardless of the mental and physical abilities they have gained through evolution. Despite becoming civilized, the male of the species is still driven by its hormonal need for sex, regardless of who or what it takes to satisfy that drive.

Then again, perhaps talking about a sexual contract is just too complex an idea to be correct. Perhaps appearing "civilized" is the human male's equivalent to the colourful displays put on by many species of male birds, or the equivalent to the size gains necessary to be a successful hippo harem owner. Perhaps someday someone will study this further and come up with an even better explanation of why men are pigs.

Part 2: 1980 to 2010

9) My Early Career

"People ought to be measured not by the mistakes they make, but by how they respond to those mistakes and by the mistakes they repeat."

J. F. Sexton

Just as my post-graduate program was an accident, I started my career through happenstance. I needed money to support myself while finishing my thesis and so I applied to work at the local tax centre in the fall of 1976.

At that time, there was only one office that processed tax returns and so it was a very busy place from mid-January to early summer. Because I scored well on the aptitude test that was a requirement for employment, I was given the task of checking tax returns for simple things like addition errors and invalid or missing receipts. While that does not sound like much of a reward for doing well on a test, it was certainly better than pushing carts around or opening mail. The pay was relatively good for early 1977 and I even got promoted up one level based on the quality and quantity of work that I completed.

I have always tried to learn something from every person who has been my boss. In this case, I vividly remember my first supervisor and her boss and from both of them I learned valuable lessons.

What I learned from that supervisor were things that should not be done. She was a nervous type who had difficulty making decisions which caused work to be delayed and put additional burdens on her own supervisor and the staff. From her, I learned the value of making a call one way or another. I learned that it is sometimes better to be wrong than to dither and continually second-guess yourself.

From her boss, I learned something quite different. When I first started the job, I had considerable difficulty following the rules that were laid out in our manuals. Often I would see things that were acceptable by the rules but that I knew were incorrect under the law. I found it difficult to ignore such errors. Today, I know that these small errors are normally picked up elsewhere but in my innocence I spent a great deal of time and effort to catch them. That time spent was directly reflected in fewer returns checked than ought to have been the case. After a couple of weeks, I was called into the office of my supervisor's boss and was told in no uncertain terms that I would be let go if my work did not improve. So I turned things around and I learned the value of clearly expressing to others the consequences that would arise from their actions. In later years, I would value the friendship that I developed with this person even after I rose much higher than her in the organization.

I was only employed that year for a few months and then, as expected, the filing season ended and I focused on finishing my thesis. But I had achieved good enough results that I was re-called for the next filing season at a new and higher-paid level.

In 1978, I was given the more responsible task of checking returns that reported foreign income and taxes. Normally, these returns contained mountains of documentation and receipts. But I loved the challenge of following the paper trail and verifying every claim made. And despite often finding errors in the mountains of paper that others might have missed, I still managed to go through more returns than most of the other people with that task. After a while, that caught the attention of others and it would earn me another new challenge the next year.

To meet that new challenge, I was re-called later that same year to study the assessment of returns whose filers had business, or businesses, that spanned many provincial jurisdictions. These were always complex returns mostly completed by accountants. Despite that, it was still necessary to check them just like any other return. Because the main computer systems were not programmed at that time to make the complex tax calculations required, we had to learn to calculate these taxes by hand with the assistance of a desk calculator.

Thankfully for future employees, the main computers were eventually programmed to do this task, but that future development taught me another extremely valuable lesson that has never left me.

Most of the people around me that year thought that they were irreplaceable based on their high skill and knowledge level. However, it ought to be plain today that no matter how complex the task, if it is driven by rules and not judgement, then it can be computerized or robotized, thereby making the human component redundant. Young people should remember that difference before making any hasty decisions about future education plans.

So I worked throughout 1979 and into 1980, checking these types of returns and saw the first generation of desktop computers introduced into the office to speed our production. Those computers used 7.5 inch diskettes and were monstrously slow by today's standards. The visual output was a scrolling ticker-tape like display showing what had been keyed and the results were output to a printout. But it was still more efficient than doing these calculations by hand despite the fact that only a couple of these machines could be bought (they were hugely expensive) and we had to queue our work to be processed by the operators.

It was at this time that the federal government started to pursue a policy of decentralizing the work it did from Ottawa to other areas of the country, particularly regions that needed employment opportunities. While this policy never made good business sense, for the people that gained employment it was, no doubt, a blessing. It is a good example of how political decisions can often be seen as both good and bad depending on your perspective.

Offices had already been opened in three other locations, Winnipeg, Surrey and Shawinigan, but in the early part of 1980 word came out that the next office would be opened later that year in St. John's. Since I had no other career prospects and the rest of my friends all thought it would be a good thing to at least try, I applied for a number of different positions in the new office along with most of my buddies.

I managed to qualify for several positions through the competition process then employed by the civil service. That process has gradually changed over the years but it has always been based on merit as measured by some sort of evaluation, written, oral or by previous performance reviews. Not all the competitions were held simultaneously since the requirements for each type of position were different. Therefore, although the competition for the job I really wanted was still not finalized, I accepted the best position for which I had received an offer and soon found myself heading to St. John's,

Newfoundland, to find a place to live.

I had just met the person who was to become my life partner. The idea of moving so far away left me wondering if he would come with me or not. I knew he had mixed feelings about it because his mother was mentally ill and alone with no other family for support. In the end, he did join me a month after I settled in and actually found a job within a few weeks of arrival. Being a francophone allowed him to get a job ahead of many others because of his fluency in both languages. Oddly enough for a province that one might think is largely English speaking, there are several islands off the coast which remain a colony of France and those folks frequently come to St. John's to shop. Therefore, the need for French speakers to provide services to those visitors, while not great, is there nevertheless.

In a strange twist of fate, the French spoken by those folks was the same French that I tried to learn back in high school and I better understood them than the francophones I had met in Ottawa. Many years later, when my partner and I visited Paris on vacation, there was a person standing in line with us who said in perfect Parisian French to my partner how well he "spoke French for an Englishman". My partner was deeply insulted but I just had to chuckle. It was even more amusing when I never had any problems ordering at restaurants in Paris while he had to be asked frequently what he was trying to order.

But at the time when I moved to Newfoundland, it was nothing like I had ever experienced before. After landing and checking in to my hotel, I called for a taxi and faced my first exposure to a heavy bayman's accent. I could not even understand what the driver was asking. After several embarrassing requests to repeat the question, I finally just guessed and told him my destination. It was, in hindsight, a prequel to Paris.

Some years later, I was talking with a group of colleagues at coffee and mentioned how unique the society was in Newfoundland. Based not just on the accent, but also on the use of terminology and phrases heard only there, the language spoken on the island is truly a unique dialect of English. When you get out of the big cities, it becomes more and more difficult to understand for mainlanders like myself. But my reference to a "unique society" was not taken well by one of the folks sitting around the table. He was a Quebec nationalist and was visibly angry, telling me that I did not know what I was saying and he left the table. I have not seen this man for a long time now but it is interesting to observe how a phrase being claimed as a symbol by one group can be so vehemently defended when it is used to describe another group.

I understand the psychology of the situation, but I do not understand its logic. Attributing a characteristic to something does not, in fact, diminish its meaning with respect to another thing. It is a different thing to say that neither group is different or unique, implying something akin to "they all look alike". That can be derogatory. But saying that both have unique characteristics is simply stating the obvious.

St. John's in 1980 was a major port but the city had only about 100,000 people, including the suburbs. It was the largest city on the island of Newfoundland but the population centres were widely separated. I learned how big the island was when I went to Corner Book later that year. It took 12 long hours to get there along the Trans-Canada highway.

In those days, there was 20% or more unemployment in the city and a higher rate on the rest of the island. That was part of the reason the tax centre was being opened, to provide some much needed employment.

After I found an apartment, I took a bit of time to visit the local chess club. As a result, word spread quickly that a new player was moving to the island. Put in perspective, this was like a major sports star being drafted or traded to the local team that had been near the bottom of the table for a long time. I was not a major star, but I was rated higher than any other player on the island by a considerable amount.

So shortly after my actual move, some of the other players drove me to Corner Brook to play for Newfoundland in the Atlantic Open Chess Championship. To the unpleasant surprise of the players who had come from Nova Scotia and New Brunswick expecting an easy tournament, I entered as the highest rated player and went on to win the tournament.

The day following the end of the tournament, the St. John's

Evening Telegram proudly noted that for the first time a "Newfoundlander" had won the Atlantic chess championship. I still have the clipping from the paper. It was an interesting feeling to suddenly become a native son after living there for only three months.

With apologies to the real native sons of Newfoundland, I found my three years in St. John's to be somewhat depressing. On the other hand, perhaps a Newfoundlander would be perfectly suited to appreciate my feelings of being so far away from family. I do not think I have ever met a Newfoundlander living on the mainland who did not miss the island and want to return home.

It seemed to me that the entire island was run on the basis of family connections, not in a bad or corrupt way, but in the powerful bonds that I saw in society there. All I heard day after day was "see my cousin for that", or "my brother-in-law can do that for you", or even "missus up the road is really good at that". I had to learn what "missus up the road" meant before I knew it was a reference to some neighbour a few doors down. These informal links got things done. Without this type of reference, it was always a challenge to find the right person or service.

The worst thing, though, was the food. I am not a sea food lover and so the choices became more limited and more expensive. In those days, fresh fruit and vegetables at the supermarket were impossible to get. All I saw were things with a little brown around the edges and lots of turnips and cabbage. Even the cafeteria at work served things like fried bologna or a local favourite, "chips, dressin' and gravy", for lunch. I have visited the island a few times since I left, but I do not know if the new prosperity has brought change to the food because my visits were spent eating in restaurants, not shopping for groceries.

On the other hand, the best things were the people and the land itself.

The island of Newfoundland is starkly different from anywhere else in the country. Much of the island is barren of trees, a legacy of shipbuilding in the province for many centuries. As a result, much of the topsoil is also missing and bare rock shows through the terrain everywhere. It is no wonder that folks call it "the rock". Where the terrain becomes more rugged and even mountainous, forests still remain and the scenery is amazing. Lakes are not called lakes, but ponds. Most of them are rather shallow. Moose abound although they are not native to the island. In fact, they are somewhat a pest because of the traffic fatalities caused each year when cars hit them on the Trans-Canada highway at night. There are no snakes on the island, so those who fear them need not worry.

There are also no Beothuks. Those first inhabitants of the island were wiped out by the arrival of the Europeans mostly through the spread of disease. But memories of them abound.

Other memories can be found on the Northern Peninsula of the island. It was there that the first Viking settlement in North America was founded and its remnants can still be seen. While the Vikings did not discover North America any more than Columbus did, their bravery crossing the Atlantic in craft much smaller than used by Columbus remains astonishing.

The islanders who live there today are incredibly welcoming and sharing. I was treated well by everyone I met. The only thing that I noted after a while was that I was always treated as a "come from away". Opening my mouth gave me away as someone who was not a real Newfoundlander and, as a result, I observed subtle changes in the behaviour of people dealing with me. It was not nasty, but there was often an air of "oh dear, I'll have to explain this to him". I cannot even say it was condescending, just a sense of fatigue explaining to mainlanders how things worked. Then I would see the same patience taking over that I saw when cars would stop on some main street downtown for a duck with ducklings to waddle across the street. Islanders are not lazy by any means but they always seemed to have a more relaxed attitude. I would describe it best as, "if it doesn't get done today, it'll get done tomorrow" type attitude. In my retirement, I think I finally appreciate this sentiment.

But this proved somewhat problematic in the work environment. Contrary to most people's impressions, it is possible to get fired from the civil service and I had to do so to one individual because he simply could not adapt to the rules and pressure of production. It was the only occasion that I ever had to dismiss anyone and it was incredibly stressful for both sides. For those who have been let go, never think that it is easy for the boss either. The process dragged on for months which is one reason why many managers are reluctant to go that route. In the end, my record keeping upheld the decision when the union appeals went as far as regional headquarters. I did learn, however, the importance of keeping records and never failed to do so later in my career whenever I had the slightest indication that it might be required. Thankfully, I never again faced a similar situation and I happily shredded the personal notes I had kept when my retirement drew near.

During my time in St. John's, I held three different positions moving up each year to a more responsible and better paying job. Two of those jobs were supervisory and at the end I held a management position. However, it was obvious to most that the purpose of moving the processing of returns here was to employ local folks, thereby helping to reduce the unemployment figures. Even by the second year of operation, some mainlanders were wining positions back in Ottawa and being replaced by the now experienced local folks. I joined that migration in 1983 with truly mixed feelings.

Overall, my time in Newfoundland was an incredible learning experience. I gained a lot of knowledge about how the Department worked because the office there was a small processing centre and everyone could compare notes. Being able to see the whole thing, rather than just your part, was invaluable. Although all knowledge ages and tends to become obsolete or invalid over time, certain fundamentals never lose their importance.

One very important thing that I gleaned both from my university days and from this office was that small operations allow people to learn from everyone around them. The pressure of being big prevents this type of informal, but critical, learning. The advantage of being small was to have a definite influence on my thinking later in life.

While in Newfoundland, I won every chess tournament I entered and have quite a number of trophies to show for it. Because of my record, I became the target of every player's hopes and ambitions which always carries with it both pressure and fun. The one game I vividly remember losing was in a simultaneous exhibition that I gave at a school outside of St. John's. One of the teachers was running a very successful chess program for youth on the island and asked me if

I would visit his home school and give a demonstration. I played about 20 students simultaneously and easily wrapped up most of the games. But one game dragged on for a bit longer. The young lad was deeply focused on what seemed a real chance for a bit of fame and glory. I knew that I was winning but I did not think he knew it. In any case, my hand sort of slipped and I made a mistake that caused his face to light up as I had never seen before. He methodically took advantage of that mistake and won the game. It was the last game to finish and his friends crowded around to congratulate him. His teacher was very happy and thanked me for my mistake.

I also picked up photography as a hobby. As with most things that I have taken up over the years, I immersed myself in all its details. I spent a great deal of money and established my own darkroom, doing negatives and prints in both black and white and colour and even colour slides. I took a lot of photographs around the Avalon Peninsula and a number of them still hang in my home. My own personal favourite is a picture of the old cannons being fired on Signal Hill. I managed to catch the full explosion, smoke and red fire, coming out of the barrel. I made a 16x20 print from it and still think of it fondly as probably the first time I managed to "capture the moment".

I still have two pieces of art that came back from Newfoundland with me. One is a pen and ink drawing signed by a local artist of Cabot Tower. The tower sits on top of Signal Hill overlooking the city of St. John's. It is a large drawing, being about 16x20. But the other piece is very special to me. My staff gave it to me when I left. It is a small signed water colour showing a typical street scene in St. John's. It sill hangs proudly in my house.

There was one other experience I had in Newfoundland that not many folks have shared. I was privileged to serve on a jury. That sense of privilege was not shared by many of the other potential jurors, but I thought I was fortunate because it allowed me to participate in our justice system which was not only my civic duty but it was also an incredible learning experience. Actually, I served on two juries during that process since I was one of the two people selected to sit on the "mini-jury" when the lawyers challenged potential jurors for cause. It is illegal in Canada to discuss the jury's deliberations so the most I care to say was that the trial was for a serious crime and I remember feeling the weight of responsibility throughout the process. But without the participation of ordinary citizens, justice cannot be served.

10) Government and Taxation

"The rule of law may be better than the whims of a dictator, but the law is heartless and cold and can never replace the human sense of justice."

J. F. Sexton

Government is what it does.

Good government performs the duties that are demanded by the citizens of its realm. When individuals cry out, "why doesn't someone do something about this?", that someone is almost always government.

Bad government performs the duties that are demanded by its leaders. And the power of those leaders almost always encourages them to demand things that are self-serving and often detrimental to the general well being of society.

All governments establish rules by which they can and do act and to which they are held accountable. Good rules are those that protect the individual from physical and economic harm. Bad rules allow one group within society to impose its will upon others; a will that is often contrary to the beliefs, values and well-being of those others.

Every rule costs money to enforce. Governments can physically create money but the value of such created currency declines as more and more of it is printed or struck. In truth, money is simply an abstract value of the goods and services that are exchanged. Put another way, instead of bartering a goat for a few bushels of wheat, individuals offer coins or pieces of paper (money), which represent the value of the goods or services being exchanged. That represented value can then be traded for something else in the marketplace. Faith that the currency is based on the actual value of products and services being exchanged is the sole basis for our monetary systems today. The loss of faith in a currency's basis weakens its perceived value.

So to maintain faith in the currency, governments must obtain revenue from their citizens to enforce society's rules instead of just printing notes to pay the bills. And normally, instead of being paid when the rules are enforced, governments predict their needs through a budget and demand payment in advance through various systems of taxation to ensure that all citizens have contributed equitably, although not necessarily equally.

Methods of Generating Revenue

It is a commonly accepted notion that those with greater wealth and who have, therefore, more to be protected, ought to contribute more to society's operations.

Based on that principle, the idea of taxing income was born. By paying a percentage of income, the wealthy pay more in absolute terms, despite being taxed at the same percentage as others. Over time that was modified by the introduction of progressive rates of taxation whereby earnings in excess of certain thresholds were taxed at ever higher rates. It was thought that the highest income earners could afford to pay a greater percentage of their top marginal earnings because, unlike the poor, they did not need all their income just to pay for essentials like food and shelter.

Let us examine the idea of paying a percentage of income, ignoring the notion of a progressive rate for a moment. To put it in terms of a parable, a spoken vehicle much favoured by politicians, rather than everyone contributing one chicken equally, everyone contributes some percentage of new chicks hatched (income).

Is this truly equitable and fair? What about the farmer who has a thousand chickens but trades or eats all the eggs produced rather than letting them hatch and does not, therefore, have any income (new chickens) on which to pay taxes? That farmer has used a clever means to legally escape taxation much like the use of so-called loop holes in many tax systems. Compare that to another farmer who has ten chickens, all of which produce ten chicks. That small farmer trying to increase the flock will be taxed far more than the large farmer because the small operator could not take advantage of the same loop-holes.

Based on this example, is income always a fair measure of what a person ought to contribute to the maintenance of society? A famous wealthy individual once said that "taxes are for the little people" and this example well illustrates that sentiment. Large corporations with billions in revenue can often legally escape contributing to society through the careful study of the rules and avoiding circumstances under which they might be required to pay.

Is taxing wealth any better?

Taxing wealth is how most municipalities operate in Canada through a system of property assessments. Based on the value of the property, the citizen is taxed a percentage of that value. In principle, it is thought that a person with greater or more valuable property must be able to contribute more to society than someone without such property.

Real property, though, is often acquired through a lifetime of hard work and savings and therefore taxing property is actually a form of double taxation when the original money to buy the house, and the land on which it sits, was already taxed as income. Furthermore, it is superficial to assume that this form of wealth means that the property owner has an income stream that is commensurate. In fact, many retirees have greatly reduced income despite having a fully paid mortgage.

Furthermore, charging for things such as garbage collection and disposal based on the value of the property being served is a little like charging a well-dressed person more for a tomato than someone who looks less well-off. Does that make any sense at all?

Knowing that taxing either income or wealth can have unfair consequences, many governments have adopted a system of taxing monetary transactions through a sales tax. The principle is that when money changes hands, a portion of it should be contributed to the public good. The more money that a person has, the more they will spend and thus pay a greater share of the public burden. This works very well and fairly until exceptions begin to creep into the system or society's members become chronic savers.

It also breaks down and becomes a burden when governments continue to maintain all the other forms of taxation. In those cases, it becomes just an additional way to generate revenue without addressing the fairness issue. Further, allowing business entities to offset the sales taxes they pay with the sales taxes they must collect provides an escape clause that can only be closed by taxing them in some other manner.

There must be balance and fairness in any system of taxation. Arguments about establishing the same rate of taxation for everyone, a so-called "flat tax" on income, make sense only when the definition of income is strengthened and not subject to exemptions or special credits. Sales taxes make sense only when applied to absolutely every financial transaction with no credit for the payment of sales taxes and no exemptions for the so-called essentials.

It must be concluded, therefore, that the manner in which governments raise income today is fundamentally flawed.

Government Spending

What about the manner in which governments spend their income?

Governments provide for many things, some of which are consumption based but many are not, like justice and defence. In most cases, these non-consumption based services cannot be provided in any practical manner by any other body.

Other fundamental services that serve the common good are things like roads and schools. Having roads and bridges facilitates the working of society. Universal literacy is a good thing and, whether members of society have children or not, it is a benefit to all when all can read and write.

Most of the world includes medical care as a fundamental service guaranteed by government. Access to medical care is also a good thing to have, if only for those few times of need.

But even when governments rely on the private sector for the provision of things like natural gas, electricity, communications and pharmaceuticals, these services cost money for governments because of the regulatory regimes they must maintain to protect the public.

Governments ought to provide only that which is deemed necessary to the proper functioning of society. But it is the definition of what is necessary that normally proves difficult. And clearly that definition will vary from one community to another.

At the end of the day, though, every government makes public decisions on how it spends the money raised from its citizens. But there are many ways in which governments squander the revenue that is owed to them. Through the passage of special tax breaks, they simply forgo revenue that they would otherwise have been entitled to receive.

The Granting of Tax Dispensations

All governments wrestle with the issue of revenue to pay for the things that are important to society and that they are expected to provide. They also wrestle with the issue of rewarding certain groups within society upon which their power depends.

The provision of tax exemptions to powerful sub-groups within society is always contentious and so these exemptions are often hidden in regulations and cloaked in complex legal terms making them difficult to either find or decipher. At the opposite end of the spectrum, some exemptions intended for widespread use by certain segments of the voting public are proudly broadcast as vote-gaining bribes.

The tax-loophole, or the tax incentive as politicians like to describe it, is legal permission to avoid contributing to society if you behave in a manner approved by the politicians or espoused by certain groups. It is a thinly concealed bribe. But it is not a bribe paid by the politicians themselves, it is paid by those who cannot, or do not, choose to behave in the manner being encouraged. Those unfortunate citizens must pay extra so that the favoured can escape taxation.

Every loophole represents forgone revenue and ought to be considered, therefore, as a cost by government. And these costs achieve very little in terms of what government ought to be providing. Loopholes only help individuals and corporations avoid paying taxes while still benefiting from everything else that government provides. And governments cannot guarantee that the money saved by those entities will be used in a socially responsible manner.

Taxation is the means by which citizens pay for the services they demand. Nothing is free. But the layering of complexity that is the result of social manipulation through exemptions and special deductions in the tax laws is inexcusable. Giving away the right not to pay taxes as an incentive to behave in certain ways perverts the basic foundations of society. Why should someone still benefit from the common good if they can avoid contributing to it by behaving in special ways approved by government.

Living Beyond Its Means

When politicians give away the right not to pay taxes to too many people and corporations and do not, therefore, have enough revenue to pay for the services they have promised, they resort to one of two solutions, borrowing from creditors or printing money.

Borrowing only postpones the need for revenue since those loans must be repaid in due course. In fact, borrowing guarantees the need for even more revenue in the long term, not only to fund the ongoing cost of the services for which there was insufficient revenue to pay initially, but also for the repayment of those loans with interest. It is a potential disaster if the revenue base does not increase since either the tax rate would then have to be substantially increased or services would have to be drastically cut. Therefore, borrowing should be seen as a short-term solution to be used in emergency situations only.

The other alternative, printing money, is a recipe for immediate catastrophe. Such money has no basis in the real economy and, as such, has no worth. It causes external entities to look upon the currency as a whole as having greatly reduced value and directly affects trade.

What Can Be Done

All members of society have an obligation to contribute to society's general well being, at least to the extent that they are able. But human nature is greedy and self-serving. Politicians know this and are very good at seeding their messages with promises of money for this and that when they know that the cost of such things must eventually be paid by those that receive it. They know that the promise of some short-term gain is irresistible to the masses.

Are there ways to greatly reduce the ability of politicians to tinker with the tax system and ways to reduce the ability of the truly wealthy to avoid their fair share of society's costs?

Full transparency in the budget process would help all members of society see how much is being spent and on what. Such transparency is impossible in the budgetary process employed by most governments today. It is impossible because of "budget secrecy". That secrecy is deemed necessary so that private interests cannot take undue advantage of planned incentives, or loop-holes. However, if the open discussion is only about expenditures and everyone is a participant, no one gets any particular advantage. On the other hand, everyone gets a chance to challenge what is being spent, either because it is too much or too little. And because of potential challenges, any investment in sectors where government spending is being proposed becomes highly speculative.

Equitable taxation requires two things. First, it requires a consensus around spending as discussed above, and then it requires citizens to accept that they have a duty to contribute their fair share to the maintenance of society. Instead of seeing the avoidance of taxes as a popular game, such avoidance should evoke moral outrage.

However, most citizens and corporate entities clamour for ways in which to avoid taxation. They do so because they see others gaining through exemptions and simply want to be treated equally. The only solution would appear to be the elimination of all these exemptions and loop-holes so that no one gains advantage. The only system of taxation that comes close to this "fairness" today is the sales tax. With some modifications, it might be a possible solution.

Modern sales taxes are applied to retail sales and, in some cases, to services. But if society is to drop all other forms of revenue, then should not such taxes be applied universally. When an employee receives wages are they not a payment for services? When a manufacturer buys materials for the factory, is that not a purchase? At each step, if a low rate of taxation was applied then society would surely realize enough money to fund the things that it must provide and no one could avoid their share of the cost. It would take some effort by economists to determine what rate is required, but when applied universally surely it must represent a smaller total amount than most folks pay today.

An additional benefit to this scenario is that most individuals would never again be required to file a tax return. The taxation of individuals whose income is based solely on wages would be administered and collected as a "sales tax" on their gross income by their employer without the need for further paperwork. Businesses of all kinds would have to file a statement of gross revenue and remit the sales tax collected on that sum. There would be no deductions, and therefore no loop-holes, to be applied. This "simplification" would also mean a very much smaller tax bureaucracy to administer the law.

With a system of transparent expenditures and a reasonably equitable system of raising revenue, what about achieving a balance between the two? Reducing the possibility or at least the scope of either deficits or surpluses would be a good indicator that the system had achieved some degree of balance.

Governments are fairly good about keeping the books. Certainly they are better at recording what has been spent than predicting what will be spent. Therefore, might it make better sense to establish how much was spent in a fiscal year and on that basis determine the amount of revenue required during the next fiscal year? In this scenario, if current revenue exceeded expenses, then the sales tax rate would be lowered accordingly for the coming year. Conversely, if current revenue did not meet expenses, then the coming year's sales tax rate would be adjusted up so that the current deficit and the cost of borrowing to cover that deficit would be fully paid by the end of the next year. That would eliminate any need for long-term government debt.

The ongoing remittances from the sales tax would be used to pay for current operations.

There are interesting and enticing possibilities created by this scenario.

Politicians would have to be mindful that constituents would be on the hook for whatever they approve and be prepared to accept the consequences of increased spending. They might also wish to generate lower taxes through the cessation of certain programs and services. It would no longer be possible to simply make vague promises about lowering taxes without first acting to make those things a reality. The "easy way out" of simply promising lower marginal rates would be impossible.

78

On the other hand, if citizens demanded something, they would have to be prepared to pay for it in the following year. If they wanted to pay less, then they must reach a consensus around some service that they wish to see discontinued. However, if they saw needed services cut without their consent, they could directly punish those that were responsible.

In a sense, it would force the conditions outlined earlier that governments be transparent and that citizens be responsible.

But, human nature being what it is, it is unlikely that either group would really want such a thing.

Government is, therefore, what the people deserve.

11) My Career in HQ

"Humans adapt very well to almost any circumstance but often resent and resist the need to do so."

J. F. Sexton

Building A Reputation

When I arrived back in Ottawa, I joined what was later to be called the Information Technology (IT) Branch as a procedure analyst and technical writer. They gave me eight weeks of training in both system analysis and technical writing skills. While much of the training I found redundant to the things I already knew, there were a couple of things that have forever stuck with me.

First and foremost was the idea that analyzing how to do things should never be a personal quest to be better than the next guy, nor should it be a quest to put down the other guy. Egos must be left at the meeting room door. To do that was not always easy but I quickly adopted a key suggestion made during those training sessions and it has never failed me.

When talking about ideas, it is never a good idea to talk in the first and second person, "me" and "you". It is always less threatening and more constructive to speak in the third person, "it" or "that". When everyone adopts the same language, the object of the analysis becomes detached from the egos in the room to the greater benefit of the end product. People who take ownership of ideas seldom produce excellent work because they tend not to listen to suggestions for improvement and find it difficult to take note of weaknesses.

The other point I took to heart was the very real complexity of explaining how to do something in totally unambiguous terms to a complete stranger. I vividly remember a classroom exercise in which we were challenged to write instructions on how to refill a stapler. As each of us presented our "instructions", the instructor followed us to the letter with the stapler and staples beside her. It was unbelievable how she inevitably ended up in chaos. It was an abject lesson in humility for all of us who thought we could write.

If you think such instructions are simple, please think back to all those things you have purchased over the years that required assembly. Try to remember if there were any gaps or ambiguities in the instructions. It is a rare case to find instructions that are totally clear where you did not have to fill in gaps with your own knowledge or logic.

When I finished training, my first assignment was to maintain the technical manuals which contained the policies and procedures for assessing the most complex individual tax returns. With each passing year, tax laws change and keeping the instructions up to date always represented a struggle. One needed not only to understand the law and associated policies, but also how the computer systems operated so that the information on the returns could be input properly.

So just maintaining those manuals was a significant task, but having used them for a number of years, I felt they could use a major overhaul to make them easier to follow. So, in my second week on the job, I proposed to completely restructure them to make their content more accessible and easier to read, particularly for new staff.

I did not know until later how nervous my supervisor was about letting a rookie attempt such a task. He let me begin but wanted to see how I was approaching it after a couple of weeks. In secret, he took this early work to a veteran writer who commented favourably on what I had finished and proposed to do. Thus, I was let loose to create a new version of some very complex instructions. I was very proud to learn later that this new structure lasted for many years until the paper manuals were finally discontinued in favour of electronic computer instructions.

But, more importantly, this boldness set a precedent for me. Except for very short periods, my entire career in Headquarters would be marked by proposing new things and convincing those in authority to be allowed to do them. In a sense, I created virtually all my own work from that point forward. The boring lessons learned from the assembly-line floor, of simply doing what you were told, encouraged me to be innovative and persuasive to escape the dullness of bureaucracy.

With the success of my restructuring behind me and the confidence that it gave both to me and to my bosses, an opportunity arose to do something far more important. There was, as is periodically the case, a government push to restrain spending. As I talked with one of my colleagues who was on the programming side, we hit upon an idea that had the potential to save millions of dollars and speed the assessment of those very same complex returns that I had verified several years before as a clerk. Between us, I knew the tax rules and she knew the capabilities of our computer systems. In our talk we kept raising issues that we thought were impossible to solve by the other side. But we also kept providing solutions to what the other thought was impossible. It was a case of exploding commonly held myths about what each side could or could not do. Then with one missing piece taken from an old obsolete process to solve the last problem, we had a comprehensive solution to automate huge chunks of the previously totally manual process.

Putting the proposal together was not difficult and approval was remarkably short compared with some other efforts I attempted subsequently. I attribute the short approval process to the drive from the top to find ways to cut costs. This proposal was accidentally timed to perfection, meeting the needs of the day. But there was a lesson there as well. Timing is always an important aspect of any change proposal. People have to want change in order to be open to accepting new ideas. If they do not have the desire, or the desire cannot be created, then proposals for change are seldom successful.

The two of us who put the idea forward solicited a third partner to design procedures for the people who would, in the future, be newly responsible for this process. All of us worked very hard over the next year to make it a reality. When production was turned on, we did find a number of problems with the computer logic that were missed in testing, but our IT folks worked diligently to find and correct them. At the end of the day, all turned out well. Many millions of dollars were actually saved and the time taken to process these returns was cut dramatically. While one part of the process was subsequently altered to make further improvements, the same basic automation was still in place when I retired.

This project was my first opportunity to visit many of our field offices to introduce the changes and train staff. Being one of the instigators of these changes and therefore the expert, gave me some degree of confidence when speaking to these audiences and I began to build a number of professional friendships which lasted for many years. These would pay off as a sounding board for future changes that would come.

What surprised many was the quickness with which so many impediments to the processing of these types of returns were overcome. It was another lesson in how only the right questions could result in the right answers. The making of assumptions about what the other person can and cannot do has always held back progress. However, if you ask them the right questions without making any assumptions, the results are often surprising.

Some Leisure Time

Another aspect of coming back to Ottawa was that I was able to finally meet good opposition in both local chess tournaments and in other cities. Being the highest rated player in Newfoundland meant never getting to play someone better than myself. As any competitor will tell you, without constantly challenging yourself against better opposition, it is almost impossible to improve.

Getting to play masters and even players with international titles quickly helped me to improve my national rating. It had not changed much while I was out east. Even winning 95% of my games, occasionally drawing a few and never losing in rated competition, was not good enough because of the relatively low ratings of my opponents.

But throughout the last half of the 1980's, I steadily climbed in the ratings until in 1992 I finally achieved a master's rating.

It was what I had always hoped to achieve, but it also allowed me to really see how much better some of the pros were. As one gets better at anything, it becomes easier to see how much better the true professionals and the greats are. They make it look easy to most folks, but with eyes open, you can see the elegance behind their play. At my highest, I was ranked 92nd in Canada. However, in the world of chess, Canada is a minor entity and so that is a little like being the 92nd best hockey player in Egypt. An achievement yes, but not a dazzling one.

In the early 1990's, I also started to direct and arbitrate, or referee, some tournaments which entailed making all the pairings for each round of the tournament, recording the results and being available to rule on disputes. It may sound odd that chess players can get into disputes, but there are many tournament rules and sometimes players fail to educate themselves well enough to adhere to them. When the harsh silence of the tournament hall is brutally interrupted by two players arguing, the dispute needs to be settled quickly.

I had my share of players who got angry with me, as any referee would expect, but I can honestly say that no one ever disputed my pairings. Pairing two players, particularly in the later rounds of a tournament, can mean a good showing for someone who gets a lower rated opponent and a bad showing for someone unlucky enough to be paired with a very good player. The stakes get higher with every round. But there are rules to cover pretty much every situation and by carefully applying them, no one had grounds to complain although many were disappointed.

At that time I knew deep down that to move up further in the ratings, I would have to devote much more time to study and preparation. However my disposable time was disappearing as my career moved ever forward and new projects and challenges loomed. Giving chess the devotion it needed to continue to improve just was not in the cards.

So in 1992, I played what was to be my last rated game. I won it but against a relatively lower rated player. He was the odd man out, having no one to play in that round. When I was directing a tournament, I was always disappointed when someone did not get to play in a round, but it takes two to play and if there were an odd number of players in the tournament, someone had to sit out in each round. So I asked him if he would rather play me or accept the bye in that round. He gladly accepted my offer to play. It was, in retrospect, hardly a dramatic end to my playing career but going out on a winning note was better than the alternative.

Aside from playing chess, I did reconnect with some of my friends from Carleton. However, in 1985 tragedy struck. Today we have all become aware of how terrorism has affected the world. But back then it was rather more limited. There had been the events of the

Munich Olympics and plane hijackings, but they were distant. But that year saw Armenian nationalists storm the Turkish embassy in Ottawa, shooting dead the guard outside the front door. That guard was a fellow student and good friend from Carleton. I was stunned as were his other friends. It simply hit me as unreal. The photos published in the newspapers of his body laying in the snow outside the embassy were cruel and heartbreaking. It brought home the fact that for every picture of violence published, there is someone who is grieving.

In another odd twist to that tragic story, all of my friend's colleagues and co-workers lost their jobs as a result of this incident. They were unceremoniously dumped in favour of RCMP patrols at the embassies. In a sense, his sacrifice caused many to lose their livelihoods, a truly sad irony.

Meanwhile Back At The Office

The project to automate the processing of those complex returns took a few years to bed down and to add a few tweaks here and there. But as it was wrapping up in 1987, the Information Technology Branch underwent a significant change. They decided that they wanted an organization that was completely dedicated to keeping the computers running and up to date. As a result, they had no place for procedure analysts or technical writers. I still believe today that not keeping an integrated shop with both computer experts and experts in integrating humans into the process was a fundamental mistake but I understand the lure of "clean" organizations where issues like contracts and classifications are much easier to handle by senior executives. It was just the product that eventually suffered.

To avoid messy issues with staff that would now be redundant, those of us who were affected were released and simultaneously offered new jobs as computer analysts. A few decided not to take the offer and left the Department, but most of us stuck around. We were sent back to school to learn basic programming skills and were thrown back into the workplace as computer experts after six weeks of lessons.

It is hard to believe today that we only needed a few weeks to become so-called experts. But even the computer world was simpler back then. With my sense of logic and algebraic skills, which are the basic skills required for all programming, I had little difficulty adapting. Others were not so fortunate but they muddled through. Quite a few years later when I underwent testing to measure my executive potential, the psychologist asked me if I had ever considered going into the computer field since my aptitudes seemed to point that way. I had a good chuckle.

For my first assignment, I was given responsibility for the programs on the mainframe computer that took the taxes assessed from every return processed, added them together, and then created a summary report for the government detailing the actual revenue it had received through income tax. It also reported the total of certain deductions being claimed, presumably so the government would know how much those tax breaks were costing it in terms of foregone revenue. Quite an interesting responsibility for a new computer expert.

I recall one night getting a telephone call that the programs for which I was responsible had crashed and would I come into the office. I struggled in around 2:00 AM and, with another colleague, we pulled out the code and, in a flash of intuition, I spotted the problem within about half an hour. The documentation was correct, but there was a small slip in the typing of the code. My colleague was actually shocked that we found it so fast, but he made the correction quickly and everything got back to normal.

But that incident made two impressions on me that never left. First, I learned to trust my intuition which was really a process of logic based on the limited facts available. Second, I decided that I did not like to be pulled out of bed at 2:00 AM so I began to look around for a different career path.

It was a quick search and after a successful competition, I ended my association with the Information Technology Branch after five and half years and I became a policy analyst in the accounts area of Headquarters in 1989.

As was the custom in those days for anyone who had been with the IT area more than 5 years, I was given a silver beer stein engraved with my name and the years I had spent in IT. It remains in a display case in my home.

The move to accounts was a dramatic and, at times, traumatic change for me. I quickly found that I was not particularly welcomed by my new colleagues because I had no accounting experience and I came from an area in Headquarters that was considered spoiled with all the new technological toys.

This was a period of great change in many offices, not just in the civil service. It saw the introduction of the personal computer onto the desktop. That introduction meant the elimination of the typing pools and hand-written drafts. It also meant the shifting of responsibility for the final product from the typist to the original writer. Even today, I can still remember the howls of indignation related to typing one's own memos. Personally, I was thankful that I had taken typing in high school because it was a skill that suddenly became invaluable from that point onward. Other skills that had to be learned, such as the use of various software packages, threatened to create mutiny in the ranks because those skills had long been considered clerical and therefore beneath those now learning them. How times would change in the next 20 years.

It was surprising to me how threatened people can feel when someone is thrust into their midst who has a reputation for change. But I see now how change represents making old expertise irrelevant. It means starting fresh and equal with everyone else. When people who have been doing the same job for 10 or even 20 years see this possibility, they naturally become nervous. They fear that they will no longer be the acknowledged experts. At the age of 20 or 30, this is not too important. But at 40 or 50, it can be a blow unless you are the type who embraces change. It may be a stereotype, but people in accounting are not known for welcoming change and many of my new colleagues lived up to that stereotype.

Then again, I also lived up to my growing reputation. After a few months there, I had gathered enough information about how their field operations worked to put together a rather dramatic proposal to modernize those operations. It seemed natural to me to apply the same principles of asking the right questions and breaking down the myths that seemed to burden the thinking of my colleagues. There were so many outstanding requests to fix or enhance their existing supporting systems that they seemed overwhelmed and paralysed to do anything. So I simply suggested doing it all differently. Instead of trying to fix all the problems, I proposed scrapping all the old ways and starting fresh with new technology. It was a way to make the existing problems irrelevant by eliminating the old systems which were really the root cause of their current difficulties.

It was a bold concept, not easily grasped by all, but the senior executives sensed that it might be the way out of their current difficulties. In my presentation to the Director General, I could sense that I was capturing his imagination and when one of the older and most experienced managers interjected with objections, he quickly dismissed them and green lighted the whole idea.

It was another lesson learned. To get new and bold ideas accepted, one has to convince the right people. All too often, the people close to the problem have already rejected a lot of ideas and are not keen to accept the risk associated with new approaches. They fear that things could get even worse than they already are. But as you talk to people more removed from the problem, they are more open to new ideas and not burdened so much with the existing way of doing things. It is like the bumper sticker that reads, "When you are up to ass in alligators, it is hard to remember that you intended to clear the swamp".

In this situation, it was important to re-state the real issue, to produce correct accounting entries and statements. The problems were so great that the existing way of doing business had to be the fundamental issue. Doing business in a new and simpler way, aided by technology, was really the easiest and cheapest way to solve the problems.

This was also my first taste of making other peoples' positions redundant. The proposal eliminated many paper steps in our field operations. Clearly it was more efficient and quicker, but that also meant that quite a number of human tasks were no longer needed. It hit home as I went across the country again to explain what was being proposed. Real people were going to be affected.

In the end, no one lost a job because in taxation there are always new programs being introduced by the government that soak up the resources made redundant from the elimination of some older tasks. Over the years, I was always amazed at how savings in one area were used to pay for something new in another. It begs the question, if nothing new were to be introduced would those savings actually be realized by the people of this country in terms of lower costs? It also became an interesting challenge for field managers to re-train staff, not all of whom had the aptitude to learn new tasks.

It took a couple of years to actually build and test the new supporting systems but everything was ready by 1992. Our team was small and I was happy to see that. It has always been my experience that small teams function much better than larger ones, even when the task itself is large. As with any of life's endeavours, too many cooks spoil the broth. In reality, the core team was made up of three from the policy side and about a dozen analysts from the IT side. But the product that came out of that small team was still in production in 2010. Admittedly, it was showing some cracks by then, but for a modern computer system to last more than five years is still remarkable.

One of the key achievements of that system was that it introduced a generic type of support across a number of operations. Before that, all our systems were designed with only one type of operation in mind. Building new systems for each and every type of operation was simply an inefficient use of tax dollars. Being able to support many simultaneously was a breakthrough. Except where safety is concerned, eliminating redundancies is good whether in computer or human tasks.

A Period of Recuperation

As anyone who has worked on a major development project knows, it is just not possible for a person to maintain the fast pace and elevated energy levels sustained during development and delivery of something new. All people need something mundane to do for a period to recharge. Some take longer than others to regain that vigour and some never want to do it again, but I found the time following this project to be dreadfully boring.

It would come to be said of me that I was at my most dangerous when I had little to do.

That was a bit of an inside joke, but the reality was that my mind would start to wander over issues that I knew existed. Ideas would start to form in my head simply because I had the time to think without distraction.

I knew there were a couple of things we had left undone in the accounts project simply to limit the scope of change. So I chatted with one of our personal computer programmers to discuss what could be done. We hit upon an idea to incorporate his work with the recent changes in the main computer. It took only a short time, about a year which is short in bureaucratic terms, but we filled in the gap in the bigger process fairly quickly and easily. I felt satisfied then, that we had not left things undone.

But during this filler-exercise, I first worked with a woman who became something of a companion, in the professional sense, for the rest of my career. I did not realize it at the time, but in her retirement speech many years later, she generously attributed to me a renewed energy and faith in the bureaucracy the absence of which had nearly driven her to resign. I never thought that my endless pursuit of improvement could affect others, but I can look back now and see that it did. I hope she knows that she also brought something to me. She had a glorious sense of humour and a genuine self-depreciating style that allowed her to tell me when I was being stupid without offending. The value of having a reality-check from time to time is priceless. As both our careers were winding down, I spent many hours discussing with her what could be done in the limited time left for us. We were both frustrated in those days but the reality is that time moves forward relentlessly and she helped me to become content with what had been accomplished.

As that filler project wound up, a new Director General assumed his position in our area. He let people know that he wanted to develop a new vision for where the organization should go in the next few years. I could not resist that challenge.

But at the same time, the manager of our area left and I was fortunate enough to be asked to fill in until the job could be staffed permanently.

Life Outside the Office in the 90's

During the early 1980's while I was still living in St. John's, news was starting to hit the papers about a number of gay men dying of rare types of cancer and pneumonia. I rather dismissed it as sensationalist reporting, but it was the beginning of a terrifying part of our history and deep trauma for all who were being touched.

The 1970's were a glorious time for gay men in major urban centres. Many could finally live openly and express themselves and their underground culture in the midst of the first gay ghettos. However, neither Chatham, Waterloo nor Ottawa were among the places to develop such a ghetto. In fact, smaller communities were the centre of reaction to this revolution. And with my small town background, I found it difficult to join the party, so to speak. Gradually, though, my friends in Ottawa got me out to explore this brave new world and I was finally getting into the swing of things when it was interrupted by my move to St. John's.

I was surprised to discover that St. John's had a vibrant, but underground, gay community. At one point, there were actually more gay bars there than in Ottawa. But it was an odd existence because while the bars catered to a predominantly gay clientele, they continued with a straight facade for a long time. It was like being in some secret society in the movies because when you first patronized one of these places everyone in the bar would turn quiet until they figured out that you were part of the conspiracy.

But the very fact that the community there was so deeply closeted probably saved my life. I just did not have much sex while I was living there and was never, therefore, exposed to the new virus making its mark in every major city in North America. My career was not the only thing in my life that benefited from luck and happenstance.

Back in Ottawa, our community was devastated and demoralized. We suffered "while the band played on" to quote an American author. Everyone was terrified of the very thing that made us who we were, sex. And like almost everyone else, my sex life dwindled even further during the late 80's.

But all men know that you can only control those urges for so long before you go crazy. Our community led the way with education campaigns and open discussions about how to avoid this disease. Men, being the creative things they are, found new ways to have fun and limit the potential for damage. As the character Blanche in "The

Golden Girls" famously said, "They'll do it in the mud if they have to".

So despite the pages of obituaries in the local gay press every month, we started having fun again. In 1990, I was introduced to an institution that was flowering in those days, the "run". Different fraternal clubs in various cities would organize a weekend retreat in some remote area where a couple of hundred men could be themselves without the threat of bashers or police. I attended my first run that year along with about 250 other men. It was like being in heaven. We were entirely among our own kind and could be ourselves without fear.

During the 90's, I went to many runs across Ontario, New York State and even Michigan. It was almost like a circuit with clubs having historical claim to certain weekends of the year. I made many good friends, some of whom I still see from time to time. The exchange of small pins with club logos on them assured any stranger familiar with the symbolism that you were an honest and trustworthy friend of that club. One club whose run I attended in 1994 proudly declared that there had never been a single theft of anything at any of their previous 23 annual events. It was a very tight knit community in which you could place your trust.

That extended circle of friends allowed me to get back to a semblance of a normal sex life. Travelling to Montreal and Toronto was always a treat because Ottawa was not the sort of city that had a vibrant night life. Those trips were exciting and satisfying and refreshed the soul for the work week that inevitably followed.

Of note, the annual "Mr. Ottawa Leather" contest was first held in the early 1990's. Many of the organizers were personal friends of mine and I established a private computer network for their use. In return, they asked me to be a judge in the 1995 contest which was an incredible experience. But the notion of people strutting their stuff for an audience quickly became dull for me and I ceased even attending after a few more years.

Women have understood for a while how exploitative this can be. Men exploiting men is only different through gender, although I have heard it said that a gender exploiting itself is not as bad as one gender exploiting the other. I have to wonder about the logic of one bad being not as bad as another and therefore it must be alright.

Gay men have always been exploited commercially through speciality shops that charge double the price that mainstream stores charge on similar merchandise for two reasons. First, these shops try to exploit the nature of people to be predisposed to support their own and second, the shops know that their clients are often too shy to buy merchandise that may be in the slightest way sex-related in straight shops. While I understand that products with limited production can cost more than similar products that are mass produced, it still offends me to see people exploiting their own.

12) Nationalism and Human Conflict

"There are two kinds of power, the power of hurt and the power of ideas."

J. F. Sexton

When observing people, it would seem that humanity did not evolve as a creature that works well in large groups. When humans are in pairs or in a small group of family, extended family or close friends, they seem to be naturally generous and different ideas can be expressed without fear of ridicule or sanction.

But as civilizations arose, belonging to the same family or close group could not be used to define these new and larger groups of humans. Instead, commonalities were formed through vehicles such as religion, language, race and culture. The new groups developed shared goals and standards of behaviour. And at some moment on the time line from family group to communal group, an attitude of "us" and "them" arose. Those that did not belong or were different became inherently the subject of suspicion.

What triggered the difference in how people interact? Could it be it was the pressure of belonging to an extended group? And could that be something that humans did not evolve to do well?

As city-states arose, they jealously protected the land on which they relied for food production. When the needs of one city-state grew and other city-states did not want to assist, wars broke out. The intellectual solution of equitably sharing resources, as within an extended family unit, invariably seems to have been rejected by one or both parties. In other words, intellect and logic disappeared from human interactions, replaced by illogical conflict resulting in death and destruction.

In a downward spiralling circle, the need to be prepared for an illogical conflict was the logical course of action. A professional military class was born supported by conscripts or mercenaries whose role in society was to kill interlopers.

But why treat one individual as an interloper and another as part of your group? Are not all humans basically the same?

It would seem that the pressure to guarantee the survival of the community caused its members to lose their sense of logic in favour of violent protectionism. There was real fear that sharing might potentially jeopardize their own survival. Thus it can be argued that the evolution from hunter-gatherer to urban dweller caused humans to become even more aggressive and prone to violence than before. And with population growth came larger affinities, but the only thing that changed was the degree to which humans could hurt each other and the size of the groups involved.

If humans had remained hunter-gatherers, would they have experienced the same fears and rush to violence to protect that which they deemed was theirs? Most primitive tribes attribute ownership of nature's bounty to a higher being or spirit, not themselves. Conflict arises only when population pressures in distant groups force contact and competition. Does it not seem logical, therefore, that with six or seven billion people on this planet, the very cause of conflict is the overabundance of humans in a finite space?

The rise of the nation state and of nationalism has been second only to religion as the greatest *raison d'être* of modern war on this planet. Belief in, and loyalty to, one's country has been the motivation to participate in the destruction of other human beings for several centuries now. Before that, it was religious intolerance or allegiance to one's lord or sovereign that dragged men, not women, off to war.

It is impossible to consider war being caused by one individual who has a grudge against another, unless that individual controls a state. Conflicts between individuals are normally resolved through the justice system or, in extreme cases, by one party taking direct action against the other.

But when the leader of a state can convince the citizens of that state that they are being unjustly treated, then such feelings can often result in brutal conflict involving millions of innocent bystanders who have no personal stake in the outcome.

Why is this sort of nation-to-nation violence lawful when, taken on a smaller one-to-one scale, it would be criminal? Those who seek power know that power flows from their ability to influence the people around them. Sometimes that influence is based on fear, sometimes on hope. While hope is a more powerful motivator than fear, when they are combined they make for an irresistible force.

The fear of those who are different combined with the hopes of the masses can move entire populations to arms.

Ordinary soldiers will often say that under different circumstances they could have been the best of friends with the soldiers that they fought. Those veterans recognize that the human beings on the other side were just like themselves, loyal citizens doing what they thought was right. So, why is it that there are still wars?

There are wars because those in power convince the masses that they are being cheated out of their rightful destiny or their current prosperity is being threatened. And once conflict starts it becomes easy to find and produce evidence to support these arguments.

Even civil conflict within the nation state is usually based upon one or both of the same factors, hope or fear. Broad support for conflict can only be achieved through the use of these emotions. And in the case of civil conflict, it is often based on making one or more sub-groups within the nation-state appear to be acting against the best interests of the other sub-groups.

So is there such a thing as a "just" war? Is there a good reason to slaughter thousands, even millions, of fellow human beings who may have had no part in the activities that are cited as cause for war? The simple answer to both questions is no. The real villains are those leaders who argued that war was necessary and ordered the slaughter of other human beings without any truly just cause.

Thus, there is no justification for general war. There is only justification for the elimination of those who began the conflict whether internally or externally.

Of course, this raises a problem. Among members of the leadership class there is a tacit agreement that they will not target fellow leaders. Targeting even the most vilified opponent is never considered legitimate regardless of the cost that can be avoided, since to do so would legitimize targeting all leaders. And as all leaders argue, who would run the war if the leadership were wiped out.

It is a strange self-serving and circular argument.

The world has begun tentative steps to bring the most heinous of political leaders to some form of justice. In ancient times, foreign princes who lost wars were often simply executed, albeit sometimes with great pomp and circumstance. Alternatively, they were enlisted to be loyal vassals of the winners. As the age of chivalry took hold in Europe, the losers of great battles were accorded princely treatment as honourable and worthy opponents. But as the ugly nature of war became more and more evident, there were cries from the common folk to end the rule of evil princes.

Following the Second World War, an International War Crimes Tribunal was established to punish the leaders of the loser states. While it is argued with great sincerity that the leaders who were tried following the Second World War deserved the punishment they received for their responsibility in some of the most horrible crimes against whole populations, other equally horrible acts were committed by troops on the winning side. It should be remembered that the victorious powers in the Second World War were responsible for soldiers who committed terrible acts of brutality on human beings who simply did not do anything to deserve such treatment. Think of the fire bombing of Dresden and the atomic attack on Hiroshima, both of which slaughtered thousands of innocent civilians.

With the full realization that the following suggestion will never, in all likelihood, be taken seriously, every leader who orders the destruction of human life ought to be tried for homicide. If they have justification for their acts, such as proving that the human or humans ordered killed were evil, intending to kill others, then they should still be found guilty but with mitigating reasons.

If there were no mitigating reasons, and the humans killed were simply cogs in a great machine doing "the right thing" as it was perceived at that time and place, then the person who gave the orders should be guilty of murder.

How does one find the guilt or innocence of some leader? There is little point in having a legal proceeding in the leader's country. Such proceedings must take place in neutral third-party countries. However, even when a verdict is found, there will unlikely be any overt way to meet out punishment should the convicted leader not wish it. It would be necessary, therefore, to have a covert international force that could target individuals for punishment.

Surely it is better to target one or more individuals than to engage in brutal warfare with the death of many and the destruction of whole societies.

The logic of such limited action is compelling but not very likely to be endorsed by any current leader since it would restrict their ability to wield power.

And thus, the world is unlikely to rid itself of conflict as long as there are large groups of humans competing for scarce resources, lead by persons of ambition.

13) My Career in Management

"Change is too often driven by dissatisfaction with the present rather than aspirations for the future."

J. F. Sexton

Recognition

In 1998 I began my career as a program manager in the civil service. It was a temporary appointment because the incumbent manager of my area had moved on to another position. I can remember being reluctant to move into his office because I did not think I would be doing the job for long but the Director insisted, which I must admit was correct and for the best.

This was the time when the Internet was finally beginning to catch the attention of both individuals and businesses. It was also the beginning of the tech bubble, but that was a problem for the private sector. Our issue was how to take advantage of this new channel of communications with the taxpayer.

On my own initiative, I started to draft a white-paper on how to transform many of our services to take advantage of the opportunities offered by the Net. At the same time, my Director General who was new to the Department started asking around for ideas to create a new business vision. As luck would have it once again, the timing was right for my ideas and I forwarded them to his attention. He liked the draft but encouraged me to push my ideas further. I think he understood that all new proposals get watered down by authors who fear being rejected because of going too far or being too radical.

Then, as expected, my temporary appointment came to an end. It was not, however, the end of my management experience. Instead, I was moved to the E-File program which was a program used by professional tax preparers to bulk file many returns simultaneously through a secure electronic process. It was not the Internet, but one of its predecessor technologies.

As the manager for the E-File program, I had a couple of opportunities that I will never forget.

First, I went to Winnipeg to meet with the board of the E-file Association of Canada. I went to hear what they wanted to see improved and to answer any questions that I could. There was a strong consensus that they wanted to use the Internet to file their returns rather than the private data network that was currently in use. Knowing how everyone in taxation was nervous about the possible security issues associated with the Internet, I assured them that we were looking at it, but that we needed to be absolutely confident that the security of taxpayer information would be met before we could proceed.

In addition, they had concerns that the Department was picking on their clients disproportionately. Their clients seemed to get more letters demanding proof of claims than did paper filers. While I knew that all assessments were examined with the same set of rules, they had a point that when a return was checked and there were no receipts, which is always the case with electronically filed returns, a letter was sent to the taxpayer asking for proof of the claim. This apparent contradiction between equal treatment and excessive demands for proof was somewhat ameliorated in later years but proved to be problematic early in the history of online filing.

Shortly after that, I also had the opportunity to speak to the annual convention of H&R Block franchise holders in Calgary. I mostly remember that trip for the horrible virus that attacked me, resulting in a fever of 102°F, but I dragged myself to the meeting and spoke to the convention anyway. The audience was mostly concerned with the rumours that the Department was going to allow taxpayers to file their own returns over the Internet. They saw this as a threat to their business and I could understand that.

In these types of situations, government agencies are often put in the middle of a dilemma. Should they support the private sector to deliver services to the public thereby creating jobs or should they allow the public to eliminate the middle man, resulting in savings to both the individual and the government? These types of situations are never easy for the bureaucrats and usually have to be addressed at the political level.

This was also the time that the government had proposed to make the Department a separate Agency with its own Board of

Management. Officially, it would eliminate 40,000 public servants at a time of government cost cutting. In reality, the same employees were still going to be paid the same salary, just called something different and still under the broad direction of the Treasury Board. While an argument was being made that there would be cost savings overall, it was met with scepticism by that audience.

In any case, the opportunity to represent the Department before these audiences was memorable but I was never to have that chance again because my duties took me to other things once more.

My draft white-paper on using the Internet had been circulated and caught the imagination of many people. As a result, I was given the green light to set up a pilot project to permit taxpayers to request some types of changes on their previously filed returns. As it got underway, I remember one conversation with a woman for whom I had the greatest respect. She held a paper form in hand and could not see how we could ever put all the information and questions it contained on a web page. I asked her to stop and remember that the Net was not an eight-and-a-half by eleven medium like a piece of paper. She paused for a moment and I saw the light go on. She went from there to design an excellent online form that condensed much detail into a very user friendly format. It is hard now to think of people and businesses that were not Net-aware, but the mental adjustment was very real and difficult for some at that time.

For setting up the pilot, I was recognized with two awards. In late 1998, the Director General surprised me at an all-staff conference by awarding me a plaque noting my efforts to improve client service. Later, in 2001, I received the Agency's highest award, the Award of Excellence for Client Service, in recognition of the success of the pilot.

That pilot had shown how we could reduce response times to enquiries from the accepted standard which was six weeks to about 24 hours. It cost somewhat less than $1M which is small by today's standards because it used computer systems that were, for the most part, already in existence. Such re-use is rare in the world of technology but the effect on the price tag was significant.

Most importantly, the pilot also showed just how technically educated the public had become since usage was high despite absolutely no publicity or effort to direct people to that channel. It also proved many of the points I had tried to make to my colleagues who were either dismissive or hostile to using the Internet. The feedback solicited from taxpayers who used the service was 99% positive and showed that all age groups and genders used it equally. While many field managers were uncomfortable with the mandated standard to respond in some way to every query within 24 hours, it forced them into a more modern "just in time" management style and, in the end, they proved themselves up to the challenge.

Sadly, the pilot system was never converted into a production system. There was growing sentiment within HQ that it was somehow unfair to treat these queries differently (that is faster) than those received on paper. Their sense was that it permitted those with computers and Internet access, a minority of the population at that time, to jump the queue with their requests. So the 24 hour standard was eventually rescinded. Furthermore, our IT area proposed to automate much of the query process that had been handled by staff in the pilot. That automation replaced the pilot system at an initial cost of several million and had a significant ongoing operational cost to maintain. But it was able to provide much of the same service without human intervention.

I have always found that a human presence in certain processes can more effectively detect anomalies when such things are a distinct possibility. It is hard to imagine that alertness and common sense can ever be replaced by computer-coded hard and fast rules. Despite those misgivings, I never heard of any problems with the new process so once again the machine triumphed over a human.

Moving On

By the time I received the Award of Excellence, I had already moved to another task. In 2000, I volunteered to take over a project that had gone badly south in another Branch. Having spent considerable time and money on it, it had been a dismal failure to that point in time and so I quickly decided to start again from scratch, or nearly so. I saw starting fresh as the only way to gain back credibility with a rather hostile user community who had expected wonderful things only to be deeply disappointed.

104

In my first few months there, I went across the country meeting with just about every group that had taken part in the earlier effort. On one trip, I found myself in three cities in one day. But I managed to show the justifiably sceptical audiences that this was an opportunity to do things differently and better. I freely admitted to those audiences that I did not know the technical details of their operations, something that they could have figured out in any case. But I told them that my expertise was in delivering user friendly support systems and that precisely because I did not know their work I really wanted to listen and learn from them. I particularly remember one field manager who wrote to me before I travelled to his office that I should not bother to come if I had nothing new to say. Subsequent to my visit, he wrote to my Director General that he thought there was still hope to get things right. In itself, the two months I spent changing people's attitudes and instilling new hope was a major victory.

For the next two years, I worked with a team I put together to deliver a new support system for these people. We piloted the system in Edmonton and the entire team spent time there to answer any questions and to ensure that it worked well for the folks. The team was relieved that the consensus of users was that it delivered what we had promised. That relief was shared back in headquarters by the senior folks who did not want a repeat of the previous attempt

But once again, I did not stay in that job long enough to see the system implemented across the country. There was considerable pressure on me to accept a permanent position at a higher salary to manage the new system, no doubt as a reward for putting things right, but after much agonizing reflection, I just could not see myself in that job.

I have seldom cared for the monetary rewards of promotion if it meant losing something more important to me. When I first changed career paths from IT to accounts, I actually took a small cut in pay to avoid the office intruding on my personal life. This time, I did not want to be limited to the administrative work associated with an executive position which, while important, was not something that I cared to do.

In fact, that decision was a real turning point in my career. It was the first time that I walked away from what others wanted me to do. I knew I was capable of doing the job they wanted from me, but it meant moving further away from the creative process of making things better. However, my decision was not well received by the Director General who, from that point onward, harboured an obvious grudge whenever our paths crossed. Like most executives, she wanted the best and brightest in her shop but unlike other executives, she resented those who did not support her career regardless of their aspirations.

Her reaction initially bothered me but I knew that what I did was the right thing for me. So I found myself leaving that Branch once they found a replacement and returning to the place I had left.

Returning to Known Territory

The folks back home, so to speak, had started to think that there might be better ways to manage the development of the many technical supporting systems that were in existence and the many more being considered. Building more new supporting systems with only small unique features around the edge did not seem right.

There was a growing sense that there was a need for central coordination of this effort to minimize the costly redundancies that were obviously occurring.

Since my name was already well known for having spearheaded efforts to build these types of systems, I found myself being placed in the position of having to design a governance regime to reduce or eliminate the duplicate efforts.

Having to put in place rules that potentially restrict the behaviour of other managers is not to be envied, particularly when you are their equal in the organizational hierarchy rather than their superior. In fact, every managerial fiefdom came out fighting for its own particular view.

There was minimal support from IT because the *status quo* benefited them greatly. It resulted in a constant flow of funds to build these new systems. They were easy to build because much of the programming could be re-used from previous efforts and therefore had less risk associated with them.

Today, the modern concept of having a business architect to

oversee this development would have prevented the problem from becoming so big. But that concept had not yet been fully expressed even in theory. We had to stumble along making it up as we went.

After much discussion, the common elements of every existing support system were defined and they became my responsibility. That may sound like progress, but it was not. Changing one of those elements was a formidable exercise since each operational area had virtual veto over any changes. On the other hand, many of those same areas were advocating changes that I could not accept without the agreement of all.

So we hired a team of consultants and they began work to identify the issues and suggest solutions.

I have always found that consultants are good for two things, and two things only. First, they can bring expertise to an issue that is not present in the organization, share it with the organization and the organization can learn from it. And second, they can give a gold stamp of approval to a new idea that would otherwise scare senior managers away. I have found that using consultants for any other purpose is counter-productive and expensive.

In one of my meetings with this group, two of them talked about a technology that seemed like a potential answer to our challenges. I took notes and began to do my own research into it. But I did not just read about it, I obtained some of the technology and installed it at home to study what it was all about.

I had already come to the conclusion that it was not enough to offer common components that could be selected *á la carte* as in a Six Sigma type approach. That type of approach can save money for an organization, but only if structural change to the organization accompanies the technical changes. Since I had no authority or mandate to change the organization, the only way to realize success was to make those common components more responsive to the niche needs of each business area. They simply would not support anything less.

So I found myself having to re-define the questions being raised. I asked people to look at how the Internet functioned. The Web is based on an elegantly simple technology. It operates using the hyper-text transfer protocol (HTTP) and the hyper-text markup language (HTML). The protocol allows computers to talk to each other in meaningful ways. When a person asks to see a web page by typing a web address in their browser, that computer sends a request to the appropriate web server which responds by returning a small text file written in HTML. That text file instructs the browser how to present the web page to the person who asked to see it. Every page on the Web can be unique to meet the needs of both the sender and receiver but the technology remains constant and unchanging.

This was a basic commonality serving many diverse needs, a fact that was to become my motto from that point onward.

While the Web has become much more complex, with many other features added to the original, like streaming video for example, its foundation still rests on HTTP and HTML. Finding something similar to manage our business needs was what was needed.

To my very pleasant surprise, such technology existed. But it was being marketed to a technical IT audience which in many cases was not interested. While the web is essentially free in concept, since neither the protocol nor the language are intellectual property, this other technology was being promoted as a commercial product by a number of vendors. Indeed, even I could see the potential commercial value in such a technological platform but the reluctance to free the technology meant challenges in demonstrating it to my colleagues. Asking a company to demonstrate its product only guarantees seeing it in its best light and generates more than healthy scepticism from the audience, including myself.

For the next year and a half, I struggled to show how this type of approach could not only eliminate much of the redundancy in our supporting systems but could open doors to vastly improve our management controls as well. However, without the ability to show it, my efforts were seen as little more than marketing propaganda.

It is often said that a picture is worth a thousand words, and my inability to show how these products worked demonstrated that principle in abundance. When one is faced with risk-adverse executives and cannot actually demonstrate how something new might work, it becomes a virtual impossibility to win over converts.

Keeping my eyes and ears open for opportunities, I found out that a new project was in its formative stages in another Branch and there was considerable budgetary support behind it. The executives there were keen on moving to the leading edge of technology to make it a show piece of modern efficiency. It seemed that timing might once again be on my side.

In an odd twist of fate, I did not have to ask to go there. I was told I was being transferred. I have never determined if that was because it was seen to be a good thing for both sides or if my home area was growing weary of my proselytizing. The reason, however, did not matter since I was pleased to go.

During the year that followed, I got to participate in many discussions concerning the vision that was being developed for this project. For most participants, it seemed like an insurmountable challenge had been set. It was a huge undertaking and, as with most projects of this scope, the odds of success were minimal.

There were a number of consultants involved and I found myself at odds with many of them since they did not seem to be offering any new ideas, just going along with whatever was being proposed by the senior project folks. Worse, it seemed as if they were actively discouraging any solutions that might shorten the project or make it easier to deliver. They always seemed to find questions that fed on the insecurities of the executives in charge. Needless to say, being paid by the day, week or month meant that they could earn more for their companies if the project dragged on.

In another awkward development, our own IT pushed its way into the early stage of the project to ensure it could steer the discussions in ways that it wanted. They had an obvious agenda to persuade the project to use the already developed components rather than explore new options.

I found that there were very few other people assigned to the project who had both the knowledge of business operations and the technical awareness required to challenge the consultants and the IT people. The few who began to see what a new approach could mean were outvoted by the chorus of conservative thinkers. It is hard for an executive to go against the majority staff opinion but it takes only one voice to show the right way, and that is normally how change begins.

In any case, my crusade was cut abruptly short. I had managed to avoid being sent away to school to learn the other official language of Canada for as long as I could. It was a sacred cow in the Canadian civil service, so regardless of the impact on me or the work I was doing for the project, I found myself packing up and leaving for at least a year to learn French.

I was told much later that my absence brought an almost immediate halt to any talk of different approaches to the project. That made me sad but I understood why. Being an advocate of change is never easy and people know that. Therefore, to take up the torch is not something that most would embrace happily.

Going Back to School

So I found myself going back to school full-time at the tender young age of 53, with my 54th birthday just six weeks away. It is often said that adults learn by doing. In this case, we were dumped into an environment that existed only in French and had to focus every minute of the day on words and sounds that were unfamiliar but were important to our future careers.

Every night for the first two weeks I went home with a head that felt like it would split open. I had never experienced headaches as severe. The stress of focusing to hear every word and trying to make sense of it all was initially overwhelming. But gradually, the nightly pain diminished and a routine set in.

In the first two months, our little group had 12 different teachers most of whom were very dedicated to their task. But when we finally got a more permanent teacher, he was rather cold and rigid, sticking to the lesson plan and disregarding areas or persons that needed more help. That was unfortunate for most of the class.

I made up my mind very early that I would try as hard as I could to set aside my analytical mind and just listen and speak as intuitively as I could. That path was reinforced when we were told how IT people had the worst track record of success in the school. Later in the term, one of the teachers told me that I did indeed come across as someone who did not have to translate everything in their head before speaking, but that I made too many grammatical mistakes.

110

If I could not eliminate those mistakes I would not be able to achieve the required level of proficiency in the language.

So I struggled every day to digest one more learning point and a few more words of vocabulary. My problems were made greater by the fact that many of the terms I used regularly in English were not available in French. Since computer technology has been developed largely by Americans, the terminology is also American. When I checked, even the Government of Quebec websites did not have official translations for many of the technical words and phrases that I wanted to learn. My teachers tried hard to help but even they were exasperated. Much of the course emphasized being able to converse about your work, which made perfect sense for most, but I was left somewhat hanging and frustrated.

As the months rolled by, the first tests were coming due. In the Canadian government, there are levels of language skills that are measured by examinations. As one's language skills improve, the level goes from A to B to C and then to E for exempt. The exempt rating indicates that you are fluent enough that you need not be tested again. I had to achieve a C rating in what was essentially reading and speaking, but only a B in writing, the assumption being that as a manager I could get others to write for me but I had to understand what I was signing.

The first formal tests were at the eight month mark and were for the reading and writing portions. There were some scheduling mix-ups and although the class had been preparing for one date, most of the class pressed to postpone the tests. I was the only one who volunteered to take the tests on the original date. I honestly did not think that one week more would make much of a difference.

To this day, I do not believe that my teachers held out much hope for me. I also believe that my classmates were somewhat taken aback by my determination to press ahead but wished me well. The two tests were scheduled back to back over four hours in the morning. All of the class had been warned that time was almost always a factor so we should not waste it on questions we could not answer.

When the first exam started, I went through the questions one by one, skipping a few as suggested. But I found that I was finished with about 40 minutes to spare. That surprised me but I went back and made some attempt to answer the skipped questions. When the second test began, I also proceeded to answer the questions one by one and skipped a few as before. When I reached the end, I had about 45 minutes left. Another surprise. So I went back and answered the skipped questions as best I could.

We were told the results would be quick since it was all computer scored. And they were correct. Back in class, the school's manager came to the door early the next week just one day prior to everyone else taking their tests with a folder in hand. Without saying anything, I knew she held my results and I braced myself for the bad news. After what seemed an eternity, she smiled and congratulated me on my success. I got a round of applause from the class.

Actually, I had almost achieved an exemption in reading. I was only one mark short of that level. Equally, I was only one mark short of achieving a C in writing which was also more than I had hoped or expected. Not only did my success surprise both me and the teachers, I believe that it helped to build some confidence in the other students who were to take the tests the next day.

In fact, the woman seated next to me said later that she had to thank me for being so supportive and encouraging although I have to admit that I did not think that I had really done anything. But success does tend to breed success and this was perhaps one of those cases. In fact, once all the results were back, everyone was relieved because we had all passed with the required marks.

The class was split between those that needed a C level in speaking and those that needed only a B level. Since the B level oral tests were now looming, those of us in the C group took a week off to allow the others to focus.

It was wonderful to be back in an English environment if only for a week so I planned to take a little trip out-of-town. It was then that tragedy struck.

The night before I was to leave, I had an accident at home that resulted in surgery twice later that day, first in one hospital and then in another with more specialized operating room equipment. On the bright side, I got my first ambulance ride which was sort of exciting. But when they finally put me back together, I had 23 metal staples on the outside of my belly holding me together.

112

The only way I could go to the bathroom was through the tubes coming out of me and I was advised that I should take the next month to recuperate. But when I phoned the school to tell them of my condition, they unceremoniously expelled me. They felt that the five weeks in total being away would be too much and that they would try to get me into another class at a later time. This was despite the fact that one fellow student had been granted five weeks away for her marriage and honeymoon. It was blatant discrimination based on my age and my perceived low-chance of success.

So when my healing allowed, I went back to the office where there was no job waiting for me. They had filled my old position with a replacement and there were many months left on his contract. In addition, I did not come back with all the required language skills and that would prove to be a great impediment in the next couple of years.

Personal Celebration and Pain Around Y2K

In 2001, not only did I win the Agency's highest award, but I won something quite different and unexpected. One of the runs that I regularly attended held two competitions each year, one for those under 40 and one for those over 40. On the surface they were like the Mr. Ottawa Leather contest but, instead of judges, everyone in attendance participated in selecting the winners. It was not, therefore, just a beauty contest but a contest of friendship and respect. I had never even imagined running for either title but that year they were short of candidates and I was literally dragged into the competition. To my surprise, not only did I make it to the final balloting but I won the North 40 title. I received well over $1,000 in prizes including a beautiful signed lithograph with dedication which now hangs in my living room.

But nothing wonderful comes without its cost.

Three years previously, I had the lowest day in my life. I received a diagnosis that I suffered from a condition that could end my life. Upon doing some research, I learned that the average life expectancy in 1998 of people in my situation was 9.2 years. I took three days off from the office to cry and get used to it.

Over time, I became determined not to wait for the medical

profession to do better, but to make an effort to contribute to that effort myself. Over the next few years, I volunteered for about a half dozen experimental treatments many of which had difficult side effects. In one experiment, I received a spinal tap which was both very stressful and very painful. In another, I was given an experimental drug to be taken by injection twice a day for a week and then repeated after three months and six months. Each injection caused a short-term fever of up to 104°F with all the associated side-effects. The last experiment for which I volunteered involved an IV injection every couple of days over a month. Each injection caused my abdominal muscles to go into fierce spasms until I suggested laying perfectly flat without even a pillow while the drug was being administered. That posture helped to control the spasms and a nurse later told me that other folks had benefited from assuming the same position as well.

I have been told that getting volunteers for medical research is very difficult. Most people fear the consequences of taking experimental drugs. There are risks, of course, but unless someone steps up there can never be advancement in medical science. Despite my own experiences, I would be happy to volunteer again should there be potential benefits and the risks fully explained and understood. As a rational person, I know that even negative results are just as important as finding something that works. The failure of one approach frees research to go in other directions.

If I have one complaint about medical research, it is the lack of feedback to the guinea pigs themselves. I was never told the results of any of the experimental treatments, except for their effects on my own condition. The nurse who whispered that my suggestion of laying flat helped others was probably breaking some ethical rules but it was absolutely wonderful to know that my determined effort helped someone else. It is my opinion that all guinea pigs should receive, at the very least, the published results of the study in which they participated. Having read a few such reports, I know they are filled with highly technical terms beyond the comprehension of most, but for putting our health on the line, we deserve at least the opportunity to sit with our dictionaries and muddle through the results.

In any case, despite the original statistical prognosis, I am still here and doing very well, thank you. And I have not really suffered to any great degree because of it although I have to admit that it has affected my perspective on life.

However, there are other medical events that have affected my work and some continue to do so.

In 2004, I developed appendicitis. Going to the emergency room, I was first diagnosed as a possible heart attack victim and whisked away to the cardiac ward. Eventually a senior cardiologist thought my symptoms odd and started poking my belly. When I screamed and jumped, he decided to have my appendix checked. As a result, I had an appendectomy later that evening some twenty-four hours after first coming to the emergency department. I was back at work three days later. However, the electrocardiogram did reveal some anomalies which was why I was first sent to the cardiac unit and those anomalies are still there.

In 2006, I had the accident at home that I described earlier. While my body has been repaired, it directly caused my expulsion from language training and would, as a result, force my early retirement. I look back at it with great sadness but accidents are just that and they happen.

In addition, I have had periodic attacks of gout although thanks to careful diet, it has not flared up in a while. I also have arthritis in the neck, which was inherited from my mother, and in my hands. I have found that stress seems to exacerbate all of these arthritic conditions (gout is also a form of arthritis) and retirement has greatly eased the pain that I endured while at the office. But it has limited somewhat my travelling. My neck does not tolerate long periods of sitting, particularly when combined with the subtle vibrations of aircraft engines, locomotives, buses or even automobiles.

But I am a survivor. I am here today and expect to be here at least for a little while longer. Perhaps it is true that having a positive attitude really is the best medicine.

14) Human Rights

"Humanity can only succeed when people feel free to celebrate themselves for who they are while, at the same time, they celebrate the good things about others who are different."

J. F. Sexton

There is no such thing as a human right.

In reality, what we call "human rights" exist only as a broad agreement between members of the species to guard against the most egregious acts of others. Human rights are really a spin on the Christian ethic of "do unto others" and were first articulated by some of the rebellious colonies in British North America that eventually formed the United States.

Prior to that, rights existed only among certain family clans, commonly referred to as the nobility, and articulated in documents such as *Magna Carta*. In virtually all societies throughout time, certain family clans have exercised power over the common people. Those in power were usually legitimized and supported by religious doctrine in various forms, including those in ancient Egypt, dynastic China, Aztec Mexico, ancient Rome and on and on.

Today, religious authority has been supplanted by constitutional authority. Inherited power has been replaced by the power granted to individuals via the ballot box, even if many of those boxes contain predetermined results. But despite the secularization of power, the majority of nation-states still cling to a basic legitimacy flowing from one or more deities, as in the American example of "In God we trust".

It is on the basis of that higher authority, articulated often in a constitution, that the modern interpretation of human rights came into existence. Probably the most basic of articulated rights is the right to life which is an interpretation of the biblical commandment, "thou shalt not kill".

However that interpretation is flawed because humans have no jurisdiction over death and thus cannot make a law to that effect. It is *ultra vires* of any human court. Specifically, no human has the power or authority to forbid death coming to another living entity. Death is the ultimate fate of all living things. Therefore, in reality, what is meant by that right is that no human should be killed by another member of the same species.

It is critically important to note that there are no exception clauses to this right in any of the original documents. The commandment in the Holy Bible does not say, "Thou shalt not kill, unless…". Those in power and those who have been grievously injured will argue, of course, that war and state-sponsored executions take place because the condemned humans are deemed to have forfeited their right not to be killed as the result of some evil action or intent. But what has an individual enemy soldier who sits at a desk done that is so evil to deserve death?

More importantly, once a right has an exception clause such as war or the death penalty, does it remain a basic human right?

If it is true that the right not to be killed is fundamental, then the rights of many are being violated every day not just by persons with bad intent but by countries and groups that engage in conflict and sanction the use of deadly force on those who are deemed to have transgressed against them. This deadly violence against people is committed regularly by police who presume guilt, by courts who find guilt and by soldiers who have no idea if they are killing bad people or people who are just doing the same job as themselves.

It would seem, therefore, that the right not to be killed is basic only so far as it is useful in supporting the power structures of the nation-state. And every nation-state that maintains a military has expressed by doing so an intent to deprive other humans of life if that nation-state deems it essential for its security.

What about the right to be free? What does that really mean. Freedom is most often interpreted by Western societies as the right to remain free from state interference and the right of citizens to choose the leaders of their state. But what state does not interfere with the behaviour of its citizens and what state does not put limits on who can be elected or even run for election?

Nation-states constantly develop rules that either limit or force the behaviour of individuals, based on a premise that the common good needs to be preserved. In addition, they make rules that forbid those born out of the country to immigrate and join the local community unless they meet strict requirements. This is an attempt to ensure that locally born persons who have been socialized in the norms of that society continue to be in the majority.

To be judged on the basis of something that one could not control, such as one's birth, is considered unfair within most societies. Is the protection of established internal social norms, and thus the definition of the common good, worth the inherent unfairness of restrictive borders? Nation-states fear that exposure to outside norms might undermine the authority of those in power. There is always a risk that the definition of the common good might shift without warning and thus make the basis upon which the powerful rule no longer legitimate. Their legitimacy is based on the votes of citizens with shared social assumptions and should the population shift in their assumptions there is no guarantee of their continued support.

To further guarantee the stability of the existing social norms, political parties routinely filter out possible candidates who do not conform to those norms. Even in the self-proclaimed capital of democracy, the USA, there are many jurisdictions that do not allow a person to run for office who is not a member of either the Republican or Democratic parties. In effect, that is a *de facto* ban on other political parties, something which is criticized by the USA when observed in other countries.

What "freedom" really means then, is the right of citizens to no nation-state interference, unless the nation-state itself determines such interference is necessary to maintain the *status quo*. And it is the nation-state that determines what norms require enforcement and who should enforce those norms. Ordinary people have little power to influence that definition.

It also means at least two choices, choices often determined by someone else, for election to leadership roles. And money and influence are usually more important selection criteria than real integrity and wisdom.

What about the right to a free press? The common interpretation of this right is the right to know the facts concerning events in society. But it is difficult to remember when the press in any country restricted itself to just the facts. By careful omission of details or by careful selection of adjectives, reporting is constantly coloured by the reporter. It is also coloured in a more sinister way by the bias of the reporter, the agenda of the reporter's sources and by the ability of some sources to control a reporter's access to information. These impediments are well known and documented.

However, one of the most subtle blocks to a truly free press is the bias of the institution itself. All press is governed by people, and those people are a product of their background and learning.

Scepticism arises when someone is presented with something that defies previous understanding. In other words, scepticism flows from the belief that the past is true and things that challenge that "truth" must be proved beyond a reasonable doubt. Often that means not publishing the observations of reporters because it would challenge credibility. And that tendency can be, and often is, exploited by those whose motives are to obscure or hide things to their advantage. The common expression, "but that's hard to believe", is exactly what exploiters of the press hope to hear.

It is commonly said that knowledge is power, but the ability to control who has access to that knowledge is the true power. Authorities depend on a press that is eager to reflect and reinforce society's norms and a press that is sceptical of anything that contradicts those norms.

Thus, freedom of the press is an elusive freedom that is met more in appearance than in reality.

Another "right" that exists primarily in North America is the American concept of "the freedom to pursue happiness" and the Canadian concept of "the freedom to enjoy peace and good government". These are quite different ideas but flow from similar deep desires to be left alone as individuals to enjoy life in peace. Is it really possible in societies that number in the millions, or even billions, to be left alone in peace and happiness? It is a utopian notion to be free from social interactions and obligations. And, as such, this right simply does not exist in any concrete form. It is just a lofty aspiration.

All of the above may sound a little cynical. But in truth, it takes only a single conflict with authorities to see how little one's so-called rights count. While the courts may, in the end, uphold those rights, individuals must battle for redemption and pay to wage that battle. Does that costly struggle not lessen the absolute nature of those "rights"?

Once a person in authority, a police officer for example, thinks that another person has violated some law, that authority has explicit permission to ignore many of the other person's basic "rights". Specifically, that authority may ignore the other person's right to be left alone, and could go as far as violating that person's right not to be killed in extreme cases. While this may seem to be a natural extension of their responsibilities, the fact that one person's judgement can legally terminate the basic "rights" of another individual ought to be of concern. Those rights can be very difficult to get back once taken away.

Police are often seen as a neutral third-party and most citizens see them as necessary to maintain society's norms. But if one is deprived of one's rights without cause even for a short time, one would likely see it differently. Additionally, there is a common belief that authorities practise due diligence and therefore a single brush with the law, whether or not it is shown subsequently to be baseless, brands the citizen as a probable wrong-doer, a stigma which is difficult to erase.

Unless one stays home without any outside interactions, one can become a target of suspicion, warranted or not. Just being in the wrong place at the wrong time can put a citizen's entire future into jeopardy. Communicating with the wrong person in any way, can add an innocent citizen's name to a grey list of persons being watched. Most people living in so-called free societies do not think about this very much because such possibilities are, thankfully, rare. But the possibility does exist and everyone must be diligent to prevent themselves from being abused by the authorities.

So are there really any "human rights"? At best, there are countries in which there are fewer abuses of presently defined human rights than in others. But that means that there is really no place on this planet where human rights, as defined today, are absolutely respected.

Perhaps it is time that humanity re-examine the definition of basic human rights in order to define a set of principles that better reflects reality and can be respected by all.

Perhaps the best starting point is to re-examine the "right to life". Rather than a "right to life", it would be a better world if everyone had the right to access freely, or at reasonable cost, the means to sustain life. Sustaining life requires clean air, clean fresh water and wholesome, nutritious food. Contaminating any of these things ought to be a violation of basic human rights. Limiting access to food or water through price gouging or artificial shortages should also be dealt with severely. It ought to be easy to identify individuals, corporations and even countries that commit such violations. Preventing violations should also be a prime consideration of governments.

What about the right to be free? Freedom should be defined as the right to pursue anything that does not physically or economically involve another human being. And if a pursuit does involve another human being, informed consent should be a requirement.

There are several key aspects to this right that require discussion.

First, at what age and mental ability can an individual give informed consent? This is something that may be best decided by the local community. Those that do not agree with the community's consensus can always migrate to another community that agrees with their opinion whether that be a higher or lower age.

Second, actions such as robbery, assault and even murder would clearly fall under the umbrella of this right since it would be unlikely an individual would have given consent to be harmed. Going to war, which is just murder on a larger scale, would only be possible with the consent of the individuals being attacked. Thus, any individual that signs a declaration of war, or authorizes such actions, without the permission of the people being attacked would be guilty of violating this right.

Finally, there are many activities in society that potentially involve more than one person. Driving an automobile, for example, is an activity for which some degree of mutual consent is required to establish the rules of the road. The application for a driver's license might, therefore, include a signed consent to those rules. Even citizenship might require a statement of consent to certain basic rules signed at the age of majority in the individual's preferred country.

All of these things empower the individual to allow or deny others the ability to physically affect them. It also denies governments the ability to force individuals to do things to which they did not consent. There would be many things that would change in a society that fully accepted the notion of freedom for the individual.

Looking at something different, what about discrimination? Whenever any human being is subject to comparison with another human being, whether that comparison is to determine who gets a job, who can rent an apartment, who gets credit or some other process, only the abilities of the individual, physical, mental or economic, as appropriate, ought to be a consideration. Listing the factors that may not be considered, such as race, religion, gender or age, will always fall short. It is only by listing the factors which may be considered that all other forms of discrimination will be eliminated.

Of course, the examples discussed above are only a starting point, but it should be easy to see that human rights have a long way to go before society can truly be said to respect the individual.

15) My Later Career

"Logic wins every debate, except when the heart vetoes it."

J. F. Sexton

In Limbo

After my failure to complete language training, my future was ambiguous. On the one hand, I was about to reach the age of 55 which was the age at which an exemption from learning the second official language was official policy; but on the other hand, despite the exemption, no executive wanted to put me into a position where I might have to supervise Francophone employees for fear of an official complaint to the language commissioner.

That left me in the middle of an age rights versus language rights dilemma. In such situations, it is almost inevitable that both sides lose.

To the rescue came a Director who suggested a third course. How typically Canadian. The Agency had made provisions for a maximum of 200 people (out of 40,000 employees) to be made "Special Advisers" if they met certain conditions, one of those being that the candidate be within 3 years of retirement. There were no special language requirements for Advisers, only that they had to have significant skills or experience that needed to be shared for the smooth operations of the Agency.

It was not easy to complete all the paperwork necessary, particularly since it meant making a case for how invaluable my corporate knowledge and abilities were, something my modesty found difficult, but upon submission the required signatures came through thus ensuring my position and salary until I retired.

The catch was that I had to sign an agreement to retire on or before the third anniversary from the date the position came into force. I did not see that as a hardship, but it did focus all my energy on the single issue that I felt most strongly would positively affect the Agency. That focus would be helpful in an unexpected way within a few months.

I should add at this point that being forced to retire, despite my entitlement to an exemption, because of failing to complete language training simply reinforced my high school disappointment. I have francophone friends outside of the office with whom I can converse and I always speak French when shopping in francophone areas. But that does not count in a merit-based system where only test results matter. I must add that I do not harbour ill feelings about the policy itself because I appreciate its importance. Coming from a minority that has been greatly abused in the past, I understand how it is necessary to be sensitive to others.

The project that I left when I went on language training and to which I now returned was very large and, typically, going nowhere quickly. Large projects require great control to ensure every piece is working to the same end. But that very need for control places burdens on people that they would not normally have to meet. They end up spending most, if not all, of their time creating paper trails and meeting with others just to check if everyone is still on track. As a result, so much time is spent on control that the real project almost inevitably grinds to a halt in control gridlock. Based on the case studies I have read, this is true for both the public and private sectors. The only successful large projects are those that are broken down early into much smaller pieces governed by a single vision of the end-state. But it is that single agreed end-state that is the most difficult to achieve in these large projects.

When I started to catch up with the eight months I had been away, other than a multitude of objectives which were labelled as a vision statement, I did not see any articulated end-state for this project. Therefore, I set out on my own to draft an end-state that I thought answered most of the issues that had been identified before I left. It was, in fact, a type of business architecture before that phrase really gained currency. The document ended up being close to a hundred pages. The early drafts were difficult for most business folks to understand because of the many references to technology and the capabilities that it could provide. But with assistance from some good writers and editors in the office, I re-wrote some sections and re-ordered others. In the end, it was a fairly complete picture of what I thought was a solid end-state solution, including which pieces needed

126

to be delivered first and how it could be accomplished faster and cheaper than what was currently on the table.

Because it advocated a number of approaches that, while in wide-spread use in the private sector, were new to the organization, it clashed with the old "tried-and-true" solutions that were being advocated. That meant it ran into a determined establishment that feared any risk.

It remains an odd idea to me that professionals engaged in developing new solutions want to avoid risk. I understand that in an environment where previous efforts had been less than wild successes, there is a great desire not to repeat mistakes. But anything new inherently requires the taking of some risk if for no other reason than any solution will also be new and untried. Taking some risk is an integral part of delivering something new and so the focus ought to have been on mitigating that risk through the development of effective testing strategies. However, with a management team in place who were absolutely risk-adverse, they would not accept any new ideas.

While I still maintain that the end-state in the document I produced would have been far cheaper and would have achieved all the objectives of the project in a shorter time frame, it was never given a chance. To this day, I do not know if that mega-project is still ongoing or if it was allowed to die the death to which it seemed to be headed when I left it.

However, I sincerely felt that the end-state I had proposed contained an answer to many of the problems then being encountered across the Agency. It was really a whole new way to approach the delivery of support services to our field staff. It proposed using common shared technology which permitted the managers of every business area to provide custom information covering each unique operational situation. As I described it to those that would listen, it was much like how business and consumers were using the Web. The Web exists on a common shared technology making it cheaper to deliver content to the end user, and while the content itself can get expensive to design, that content can be whatever each site developer wants it to be.

Simply put, the idea was to separate content from the delivery mechanism, thereby keeping delivery costs minimal. At the same time, it allowed all the stakeholders the freedom to design their own content and control the cost of that content.

When I finally realized that I could make no further progress against the established thinking in that project, I started to search for other ways and places to advocate this approach because I was convinced of its merit.

One Last Reach for Gold

By happenstance, a previous boss of mine whom I admired had just been promoted to one of the Assistant Commissioner's positions, second only to the Commissioner. I sent him a very brief congratulations and he wrote back thanking me and asking my opinion on a subject that was near and dear to my heart. We met for lunch a few weeks later and I tried to spell out my thoughts on the approach to support services we had been taking to date and where I thought we should change them to be more effective and efficient. I gave him a copy of the business architecture paper I had prepared and told him to simply change the name of the organization to his when reading it.

A few weeks later, and with much angst, I decided to take a bold approach for the first time concerning my own future. I had only about two years left and threw caution to the wind. I wrote to the Assistant Commissioner with whom I had lunch, giving him a one-page proposal that would, in my opinion, lay the groundwork for the new approach I was advocating. Included with that, I assured him that it would cost very little and there would be many opportunities to pull the plug if it were not unfolding as it should. After a short delay, he invited me to meet with him and a couple of his senior staff to discuss it.

At that meeting, I made a strong case and confidently answered all the questions put to me. A few weeks after that, I found myself reporting to work in that Branch being asked, more or less, to prove it.

I have come to understand that employers, whether they are within your own organization or not, appreciate what you offer to bring to them rather than merely wanting a job from them. It shows a degree of understanding and commitment to the organization and a desire to make it better through your efforts. While I did not appreciate it at the time, I had followed a text-book approach to job-application writing.

Upon arrival, though, I found that the organization was not as enthusiastic about these ideas as was the boss. It meant my last two years were a struggle to move things forward but I knew that progress could be made as long as there was at least unspoken support from the top.

I also found, to my pleasant surprise, that many of the people with whom I had worked years before were now in senior positions in the Branch. That meant I could speak freely to them based on our prior history. The downside to that familiarity was the unease created for my immediate supervisor who was younger and less experienced. That uneasy feeling was probably worsened as a consequence of the Assistant Commissioner asking me periodically to come to his office to provide advice on one issue or another. While I always briefed my supervisor on the questions I was asked and answers I provided, I never felt that he was comfortable, fearing that I might have said something, even innocently, that would reflect badly upon him.

My friendship with many of the other executives in the Branch allowed me to speak candidly and with credibility to them as well, something that new people often find hard to do. Knowing them and the programs they managed gave me insight into the issues that they were facing and gave me the knowledge to show how the ideas I was proposing could offer custom solutions to each of them. Addressing them as unique individuals rather than feeding them pablum based on some vague corporate objectives always got their attention. I also tried to honestly evaluate whether this approach had the potential to bring large or not so large improvements to their part of the organization. Most executives appreciate honesty over bravado and salesmanship.

As expected, I found some of the executives were enthusiastic while others were disengaged, having other priorities on their minds. This was the first managerial assignment for my immediate boss, and he found it hard to understand why all of the executives did not want to embrace the new approach. So he started to focus his attention on the disengaged rather than aligning himself with the supporters. Both his Director and I suggested that it was always better to go with your support and let the others catch up when they saw results, but I suspect he was too much a perfectionist to see that.

Furthermore, he found comfort in the rules rather than the results. Most experienced managers know to lessen their grip on the reins when they have good employees who consistently produce results. Less experienced managers often find a need to establish their authority and he was one of those. Unfortunately, that caused clashes and ill-feelings among the staff who felt like small children being constantly watched and scolded. Within a year of taking over, he had a 100% staff turnover, including myself. While I retired, others simply left. Adults learn best by doing and then drawing lessons from those experiences. I sincerely hope he learned something about people management from those days.

It also did not help that he failed to do his homework on the technical issues at hand. Not doing one's homework can be excused if one relies on the team's expertise, which is what most managers do. But he consistently adopted ideas contrary to the recommendations of the team without a real understanding of the technology and the consequences of his decisions. I patiently tried to educate him on the subtle aspects of what he was, in reality, supposed to be leading but he insisted on making his mark with changes that were not always for the best.

This was particularly stressful for me because I had made a commitment to myself not to compromise on anything important during this last phase of my career. Normally, I had always done so when I felt comfortable that any problems created could be corrected over time, but time was the one thing that I did not have because of my looming retirement.

In the end, the objectives I was trying to achieve were tantalizingly close but I was worried by a number of things introduced into the plan that I knew to be inefficient and even redundant. However, I rationalized to myself that, rightly or wrongly, he would inherit this task and that he would learn over time what worked and what did not.

I selected the day of my retirement not on the basis of any calculation related to my pension but simply on the day that another colleague was going. I knew that I could have increased my pension marginally by staying longer but for the small annual increase it did not seem worth the stress.

I was suffering increasingly from my arthritis and had started daily prescription pain killers to lessen the effects. On quite a number of days, I just could not gather myself together to face the office grind. I had not missed many days over my career due to illness and so I had many days of leave available and took advantage of that savings. To some that looked bad as if I was simply drawing down the saved leave but the pain was real and the stress was compounding the problem. At one point, one of my doctors suggested taking some time off to get away from the stress because it was making my other conditions worse.

So it was time to go.

It had been normal to celebrate retirement with a party inviting those who worked with the retiree to a reception. However, with the increasing number of retirees from the baby-boom years, this had become less popular. I had attended quite a few of these events in the past, but I really did not feel that such a celebration was in order. I did not feel that I had successfully completed my last objective and, as in the past, that disappointment loomed greater than my many successes. Therefore, I simply suggested that a request go out to those who had worked with me on the many projects I had proposed or led for notes with any fond or amusing memories of those years.

In my remaining time, I still fought to spread the notion that there was a better way to support our programs. I made presentations to all the executives in the Branch. I developed training material and managed to deliver it to one group of analysts. And on the day before my retirement, I gave a detailed presentation to one Director's management team. It was their area that I felt could benefit more than any other from this approach. They were somewhat taken aback and perhaps impressed that I was still pushing forward despite that being my last full day of work.

On my last day, the immediate team went out for lunch and farewells. It was a simple affair and I was presented with a bound copy of the notes that had been received. As I expected, there were not a large number of notes because most of the people with whom I had worked were already gone and I knew that for many folks chipping in for a retirement gift was much easier than composing a note.

However, the notes that I did receive were truly wonderful. They were made even more special by the effort that those people actually had to put into it. There were notes from executives, administrative assistants, former supervisors and former staff.

I noted with both pleasure and satisfaction how some referred to my dedication and perseverance, others to my forceful logic. I was particularly moved by one former employee who remembered how I never passed judgement on anything he proposed. He noted that I simply asked questions that forced him to think ever harder about his ideas until he himself could pass judgement on them. His note reflected one of my most important goals with staff which was not only to encourage their creativity but also their ability to critically think about and evaluate their own ideas.

But there was one other thing that happened two days before my departure that I will remember forever. The Assistant Commissioner asked me to come to his office just to chat. I spent a little more than a half hour talking with him about life and future plans. There was nothing particularly special about our conversation except for the fact that it took place. I do not know of another person so far below his rank being invited just to spend a bit of time reminiscing. It was very special just to be honoured in this way. I would like to think that it was an unspoken acknowledgement of my many contributions to the Agency over the years.

When lunch on that last day was finished, I left the restaurant saying my goodbyes and it was over. It felt rather strange. It was very much like the poet said, "This is the way the world ends, not with a bang but a whimper".

16) Hope, Truth, Knowledge and Wisdom

"Belief in a single great truth is the end of growth."

J. F. Sexton

Hope

Hope is one of the key things that makes a person human and when it is totally absent, life becomes unbearable. Humans without hope lose all fear of self-destruction. When lost hope is replaced by new hope, the architects of that new hope become figures of adoration and heroes to be followed.

All tyrants come to understand that their subjects must have hope, if not for freedom then at least hope for a materially better life or hope to be protected from some real or imagined threat. This is essential if they are to remain in power with an obedient society.

People with a strong sense of hope will make sacrifices in the present, gambling that their hopes will be realized in the future. They will even sacrifice their own lives in the hope that their families will endure or be more prosperous. The dead, however, have no way of knowing if their sacrifice worked. But if those who remain begin to realize that they cannot achieve their hopes whatever the sacrifice, society becomes restless and starts to question the things around them. For political leaders, it is not the failure to actually realize the hopes of the people, but the failure to sustain the credibility of their hopes that has fuelled most radical change.

Hope, being so powerful and basic, has become the most exploited human characteristic by those whose own hopes are fuelled by ambition. Every politician, entrepreneur and con-artist knows this.

Politicians relentlessly try to foster the notion that only they, rather than their opponents, can guarantee the hopes of the people whether those hopes are rational or not, beneficial to society or not, or even if those hopes if realized would be catastrophic. For politicians, hope is defined as achieving power and then keeping it. It is rare that altruism interferes with this type of hope. All too often, the only politicians that truly work for the public good are those that know the end of their careers is near. Sadly, these "lame ducks" are normally the only ones with the courage to do the right thing, rather than promise a future utopia.

Entrepreneurs try to create hopes that can only be fulfilled by their products or services. Then they strive to convert those hopes into wants and needs. Unlike politicians, they do not have to do this for the majority of the population, they just have to persuade enough people to reap a profit. But the number of entrepreneurs is considerably greater than the number of politicians and if each one of them continues to create hopes where none existed before, it is potentially the beginning of either an upward cycle of growth, or a downward cycle of inflation and economic pain.

Money earned as profit by some is money that cannot be spent by others on something else. The hope of entrepreneurs is to become wealthy by convincing others to pay them the value of the goods or services provided, plus a little bit extra. That "little bit extra" is the spark of what entrepreneurs would term profit and economic growth. However, for those paying that "little bit extra", it kindles hopes of increasing their workplace compensation to make up for what they have forgone. When that "little bit extra" grows too large as measured by inflation and entrepreneurs are seen to grow more wealthy, the rest of society can become uneasy and fearful. Their hopes for a better life become threatened and, just like in politics, they will protect their hopes either through increased labour action or by closing their wallets.

Possibly the worst exploiter of hope is the con-artist. These are people who take advantage of hope without actually providing any real way to achieve the thing for which their victims hoped. They strive to achieve gains without having to provide any product or service that actually delivers what has been promised.

In reality though, almost everyone uses hope as a tool in their social context.

Doctors are loath to explain there is no hope to a patient that is dying. Instead they will frequently resort to the future as the possible source of some as-yet-unknown cure. They try to create hope when they know there is virtually none. Doctors know that without hope patients die more quickly. Hope is indeed essential to human life.

Employers use hope as a tool to maximize employee productivity, promising potential bonuses or raises if some objective is met. Coaches use hope as a tool to extract effort from athletes, promising fame in return for that effort. Parents use hope as a tool to instill self-discipline in their children, promising future success if they apply themselves. Friends use hope as a tool to bolster self-confidence in their social circle.

When the hopes of people are openly challenged or ridiculed, a spectrum of emotions from hate to despair is created. Humans resist and resent the notion that their hopes are nonsense or impossible. The easiest way to hurt someone is to scoff at their hopes. The easiest way to encourage someone is to confirm their hopes, regardless of the likelihood those hopes will ever be realized.

For those who have hope, knowing for what one truly hopes is the foundation of self-discipline. Knowing that one has achieved one's hopes is the foundation of serenity. This self-awareness is armour against having one's hopes exploited, because allowing those hopes to be created or dictated by others is the surrender of self. But really knowing one's hopes is never a simple thing, and hopes can change over time. Hope ought to spring from one's capabilities, not one's imagination, and knowing one's real capabilities is not as simple as looking in a mirror.

Truth

Truth is not a democracy. It only takes one person to discover some truth that makes all other opinions invalid. While everyone else might disagree, if the facts and logic support that single individual, then the majority is simply wrong. Constantly question things, but when one has a deep confidence that the right conclusion has been reached, persevere in the face or ridicule and scorn. Remember that every great advancement of humanity has been made at the expense of widely accepted assumptions.

For humans, the senses reveal truth but when those inputs are interpreted by their bias-laden minds, the outcome is often false.

For example, everyone can see points of light in a clear night sky. That there are lights in the night sky is true. But humanity has wrongly interpreted what they were for millennia. Even when they were "certain" that the objects were stars just like the Sun, they suddenly discovered that many of those stars were actually galaxies containing billions of stars.

Everyone has seen lightning in storms. These bright bolts exist. But humans wrongly thought that this was proof of angry gods.

The ground sometimes shakes. Since people can make the room shake by stomping their feet, humans assumed similar cause and effect by higher beings.

Noting an observation is one thing, interpreting it is another.

Great truths are usually not. Over time almost every great revelation has proved wrong, particularly those great truths that have demanded uncritical acceptance enforced by physical sanctions. One need only examine the Inquisition to see this in action.

Great ideas may seldom be great truths but they can still inspire. It is not necessary to find absolute truth to inspire progress, but progress can only come when old truths are challenged. Those challenged truths will fight to stay alive, but the new truths will eventually conquer until they themselves are challenged.

To challenge old truths requires logic and fact. Logic itself seldom achieves truth but is the most effective weapon to insert doubt into old truths. By creating cracks in old assumptions, room is made for new understandings.

Truths seldom need hyperbole to prove themselves. Stretching to find some comparative such as "the most since…", or "the largest since…" usually serves to sensationalize rather than deepen understanding. Adding superlatives or diminutives to some observation endangers the truth of the observation because things described as "the biggest" or "the best" seldom are, or seldom remain so, for long.

Finally, while truth may be an elusive goal, the imagination offers a fleeting glimpse of a possible truth that usually fades before it can be made real. But every great invention, discovery or idea has begun in someone's imagination before being turned into reality.

Knowledge and Wisdom

Knowledge is not wisdom. A knowledgeable person simply knows many things. But knowing a lot of things may help a person to gain wisdom provided an intellect accompanies that knowledge.

The absence of great knowledge does not mean the absence of wisdom. Even a small amount of knowledge when used to great advantage can demonstrate wisdom. The wise person understands there are limits to anyone's knowledge and therefore seeks out others who may have the missing piece of information. The wise person acknowledges, at least internally, that the gaps may lead to errors but understands that all answers and solutions are less than perfect. Finding and correcting those imperfections is how knowledge grows and deepens.

Intellect is the ability to draw on seemingly unconnected pieces of knowledge, extracting the crucial lessons learned and understanding how those lessons may be applied to answer other problems. Knowledge without intellect is sterile. It is like an encyclopedia sitting on the shelf stuffed with information but incapable of advancing understanding on its own.

Intellect allows the wise person to sort through mounds of irrelevant information and focus on the big question that must be addressed to solve even the greatest of problems.

It is that ability to ask the right question that identifies the wise individual. It is a key characteristic of intellect.

Ultimately, there are two great questions, "why" and "how". As every exasperated parent knows, even the small child learns by using those two questions.

The answer to "how" can often be found through the brute force of trial and error. Usually experimentation can eventually solve "how" things happen or work. But the answer to "why" often requires a leap of logic and presumption. The ability to answer "why" to the great things that have puzzled humans has often elevated those thinkers to immortal status. Newton's laws were possibly the greatest human attempt to answer why things behave as they do. And as a result of his effort, humanity still holds Newton in awe.

However, while the greatest minds have achieved their reputations on this basis, no one can answer "why" to everything that exists. It is like the question posed by the comedian Bill Cosby in one of his stand-up acts, "Why is there air?". A simple enough question that is impossible to answer. Since humanity is never likely to understand the "why" of all things, it will always be prone to reduce some answers to a supernatural source. It is the only alternative to the tried-and-true parental answer "because" as a way to end debate when there are no further clear answers.

But as humanity's understanding of all things matures, people must remain open to new ideas, never totally dismissing even the seemingly ridiculous because there may be a kernel of truth hidden there. How often has an inspiration come from the totally unexpected, the mundane or even the silly things that happen in life. Think of Newton's famous falling apple if you doubt that.

In fact, the beginning of wisdom is quietly listening to the facts, opinions and options and then applying an understanding of past events in an effort to choose a better way forward. When an individual can offer real practical alternatives that differ from conventional solutions, progress becomes possible.

At the end of the day, though, wisdom is almost as elusive as truth. It is seldom achieved without both knowledge and an intellect capable of drawing appropriately from the past. However, the wise person, while drawing from the past, never becomes imprisoned by it.

17) My Sex Life

"Luck sometimes comes to those who hope for it, but usually comes to those who work hard for it."

J. F. Sexton

I have left the other important part of my life to near the end of this book, not to keep the reader hanging, but because I have always maintained that work and play should not mix and I have kept to the same standards here.

In fact, I really never socialized with the people from work because it seemed inevitable that shop-talk would intrude, and social time is meant for relaxation and rest. On the flip side, I seldom brought up any details of my personal life while at the office despite those things being a regular part of office conversations for others. Mixing the two just never seemed right. For me work was work and took 110% of my energy to keep moving forward. But when I left the office, I really did leave the office except under rare and unusual circumstances.

I always maintained that my personal time was worth more than the salary I was being paid. Today most organizations try to encourage a balance between work and life. But I never lived to work, I worked to live. I never saw a balance. I saw the necessity of work to sustain life. For work to intrude on my own time was evil. And to make sure that work did not take away from my personal time, I ruthlessly managed my time at the office, completing things in days that took other managers weeks. I was appalled at the number of managers who had to work so many extra hours. While I realized that much of that effort was to impress and make extra money or bonuses, that just made it even more appalling.

I worked very hard during office hours. And I played very hard during my own time.

Let me start by saying that I am not unique or unusual among my kind. I use the term "kind" because I cannot use ethnicity or race to describe the sub-culture to which I belong. But using the term sub-culture is not entirely correct either. I am biologically attracted to men, have been since puberty, and continue to be today. To outsiders, this is just a behaviour or an affectation. But among men like myself, it is simply what we are. In our community, there is an entire culture rich in mostly-unwritten history, social norms and even a separate dialect used only among ourselves.

Living through our culture's emergence from dark alleys to Pride parades attracting a million people has been amazing. Observing that many attendees at those parades are not members of our culture but genuinely interested in celebrating diversity, has been nothing less than revolutionary. However, I still fear that, like most revolutions, it will be followed by a reactionary push-back. There are subtle and not so subtle signs of that reaction all around, but I continue to hope for the best.

I remember hearing vaguely of Stonewall in 1969 but I was still existing socially in dark places, out of sight, remembering the violence that lurked everywhere aimed at people like me. Unlike many I know or knew, I have been lucky over the years, experiencing only verbal abuse both directly and indirectly. Hearing jokes directed at gays without the speaker knowing my orientation was always difficult. The worst incident I ever faced was a written death threat in 1995, but I actually had the phone number of the computer that was used to leave the note, so I knew it was someone either very drunk or very stupid.

Today, the threat of violence has lessened, but among gays my age or older, there are lingering scars and many of us still find it difficult to be open about our culture not knowing who might be homophobic. I have been told that gay youth find it easier today, but the evidence of young gays committing suicide seems to contradict that.

Over the decades since I became sexually active, I probably have had sexual relations with at least two or three thousand men, probably more. In fact, during one particularly active period, about twenty years ago, I kept a sort of date book and had close to 500 encounters over the year. A number were repeats, because when you find someone of like spirit, humour and interests it pays to keep in touch.

There is an old gay saying that the definition of a slut is someone who has more sex than yourself. It may sound incredible after reading the above, but I did not feel like a "slut" because so many of the people I knew were definitely having more sex than myself.

One of the things that makes gay culture so different is our attitudes toward sex and relationships. For most of us, the two are quite separate things. But when the community tries to present itself to the rest of the world, it often slides back into a more politically acceptable posture, emphasizing our relationships. Some of our community, particularly those working hard and with genuine desire to integrate themselves into the mainstream through the institution of marriage, would strenuously disagree with that statement. But it has been my observation that many married gays still have eyes for other men, although there are some who find genuine serenity with a single partner.

Personally, I have never met a long-term gay couple that has remained monogamous. Among couples who have been together for more than 10 years, monogamy seems to be replaced by an honest and open relationship. Without that honesty, open relationships cannot work. My own partner has often picked me up late at night after I have met someone and it was too late to catch the last bus. He always preferred to do that rather than have me waste money on a taxi.

Let me hasten to say that my observations really only apply to gays, not to lesbians or other orientations. Lesbians seem to be able to settle down into relationships more easily than gay men. Does that say something about the nature of male and female sexuality?

For most gay men, sex can be a sport if it is not taken too seriously. Actually, it ought to be a sport because one needs some athletic abilities such as endurance, technique, practice and a good coach. Watching, listening and feeling are very important to becoming better as a partner. When someone does something that feels good, then it is important to remember that and try to imitate it. Perhaps, by definition, it is more difficult for heterosexuals because their partners are of the opposite sex and that means that they can only describe what feels good to another partner, not show them. In other words, men cannot demonstrate how to please a penis to a woman because she does not have one. Furthermore, most straight men do not go into great detail about their previous sexual partners not only because it would be a date-killer, but because they fear being exposed as a "kiss-and-tell".

Gay men are far more open about all things sexual because that is what defines us.

There are many sub-groups of gay men, like those into certain fetishes or drag. Within those groups, there is often a quiet and discreet sharing of notes about people to ensure that eager and open-to-learning men and men who are experienced and competent are referenced highly while others are not. Getting on the wrong side of that whispered network, means far fewer potential partners. From personal experience, both the black list and the white list can be spread world-wide and you get to know which list you are on by the number of folks who will say hi or send you a note from some far flung corner of the world.

Gays and particularly sub-groups within the gay community do not exist within a vacuum of social standards. But those standards are hugely different from the standards of behaviour in the straight community. There are many unwritten rules about interactions with other gay men. It is said, for example, that "the leatherman is also a gentleman" putting down the notion of biker violence so often associated with leather clothing. Sex in public view is quite acceptable although joining in on the action, so to speak, is not unless one gets a specific invitation. Making one's self available for sex does not imply having to accept any offer. And like straight sex, no still means no.

Gays have been using the latest technology for years to communicate interests and set up liaisons. Before the Internet became mainstream, gays were using dial-up Bulletin Board Systems (BBS's) from their home computers to share information and meet people of like minds. In those days, there were a number of networks that electronically passed mail daily around the world. Instant messaging only worked locally but who needed more when it was impossible to meet someone who was 3,000 miles away in the next 30 minutes anyway. It was the first way that gays could meet other gays without risking exposure in public and we took full advantage of it. Gay BBS's flourished and many became very profitable businesses.

I operated a free BBS in the early 1990's that went on to be a non-profit operation a few years after its start-up. It evolved into a website in 1998 and remains in operation. I learned a great deal about technology, enough to know that I could never keep up with the latest but could become competent and comfortable with the leading edge of yesterday. I rebuilt my own computers and constructed a network in my home long before the office had one. I even designed my own databases to support the BBS and the website. It was an advantage to understand these things because it meant that the so-called experts at the office could not bluff me with what was or was not possible. While I could never say so, that knowledge came from helping others, and myself, search for sex.

I wrote add-on software for other Bulletin Boards that was distributed as "shareware". Shareware is software that is free to use but asks the user to contribute to the author if they like it. And I actually did receive money for some of my programs. My most successful programs were games to while away the time waiting for a hot date. But I wrote other more serious programs for BBS use, including a matchmaker program.

My BBS and website were small compared with sites like Facebook and Twitter today. However, just after Y2K, a San Francisco gay newspaper wrote that my website was the largest of its kind in the world. I was very proud of it, but I never really considered turning it into a business.

Electronic communications have had a profound effect on gay social life. Prior to these channels becoming available and popular, most men looked for partners in bars and other venues, including venues that were frequented both by bashers and police. It's hard to imagine how two men meeting at 3:00 AM deep in a forested park could be seen as criminals, or hunted as perverts, but that is what happened. Even trying to remain unseen was often impossible. Regardless of our legal advances around the globe, the law in most countries simply does not allow us to freely live our way of life. Not being prosecuted simply for being gay was a great leap forward, but it is to be hoped that we cease being prosecuted for doing what makes us gay.

However, with the Internet, quick connections can be made without the dangers of our previous meeting places. Equally, there is no need to buy drinks all night in the hopes of meeting someone.

Businesses providing space for gay men have suffered, but the online industry has flourished.

I regularly communicate with old friends across this continent and in Europe and Australia. I regularly meet new friends the same way. I may have grown older but with access to a greater number of men, I continue to find some who are interested in me and *vice versa*. Twenty years ago, my age would have been a great handicap because of the prevailing age bias in our community, but for those who do not have such a bias the Internet shields them from ridicule for chatting with older men. And so I continue to enjoy a full and active life, taking advantage of all the things I have learned over the years.

18) Pride

"In most fields of endeavour there are winners and losers where the ambitions of some are met and those of others are crushed. Whether for power, intellectual achievement or creativity, ambition may be the fundamental driver but all too often it leaves behind hurt and failure."

J. F. Sexton

It is said that "pride goeth before the fall". That saying is meant to instill a little humility in everyone because those that become too proud often find the world around them does not share the same opinion. Everyone's fifteen minutes of fame is fleeting and is often followed by the bitter experience of rejection.

But what is pride really?

In the dictionary, for those that still use that archaic type of book, there are a number of definitions that are relevant to this discussion.

The Oxford, a bible of English spelling, says firstly that pride is "the unduly high opinion of one's own qualities". That definition fits nicely with the fall already noted.

The dictionary goes on to a second meaning, saying that pride is a "sense of what befits one's position, preventing one from doing unworthy thing" (sic). That is somewhat like the old saying, "I would not stoop that low". But there is more to it because there is actually a certain expectation that those with position ought not to be doing things beneath their station in life. It flows from the ancient notion of nobility and nobility's inherited rights from some deity. Is this pride a good thing? If all people are created equal, then should they not be expected to chip in whenever required, regardless of the task. Of course doing so would render an impression of equality, something not desirable among those who have station and power. There may even be practical reasons for not mucking-in, so to speak. They have to make decisions, do they not? And that takes a great deal of time away from the possibility of doing the more mundane tasks. It is too bad that decision-making does not actually complete the task. That remains the work of people of lesser station.

A third definition of pride is "a feeling of elation and pleasure due to action or circumstance that does one credit". It is to be hoped that everyone experiences this meaning at some point in their lives. While it is fleeting, it makes all the work, sacrifice and struggle worthwhile. The person who has never had the pleasure of this feeling, must feel terribly empty. But this feeling is also like a narcotic. Once you have had it, you want it again and again, and pursue it with an energy that may, in fact, be self-destructive or detrimental to those around.

The final definition that fits this discussion is that pride is the "object of this feeling", as in "his mother's pride". In this scenario, one may lack pride altogether in one's accomplishments but mom, being mom, still feels proud. For the object of this feeling is it then a good thing? That is unknown by definition but the likelihood is high that mom's pride may be the only pride experienced by some people.

So there are four definitions of pride.

The first two may be easily described as vanity rather than pride and that ought not to be seen as a good thing.

If the third definition makes pride as addictive as heroin, then it simply reveals another problem with the notion.

The last definition draws attention to the sad fact that all mothers love their children whether or not the rest of society feels the same way. Unfortunately, mom's love does not earn a living, let alone promote a career.

Taking another, non-dictionary approach to the word, every office extols its staff to take pride in their work. But that does not seem to fit any of the definitions above, so what does the boss mean when making speeches to the troops and inspirational posters go up on the walls? To "take pride in one's work" means doing the job well enough that the company prospers, something that benefits the owner greatly and possibly the worker also, but only if the extra profits flow through to that worker. So this version of pride is really only an admonition to work harder, with the chance of sharing in the benefits held out as a carrot.

146

Then there is ethnic and cultural pride. This type of pride, when expressed simply as feeling good about who you are and where you came from, is good. Sadly, however, this type of pride has often led to conflict. It seems that all human groups need to feel that they have some inherent advantage compared to others. No one wants to be at the bottom. Therefore, it is convenient to point to other groups and start making comparisons which inevitably lead to the conclusion that one's own group is blessed or better. And if the facts do not support such a conclusion, then facts are often invented through legend, historical distortion and imagined slights. This is pride at its ugliest.

In most of these definitions, pride is not something of which to be proud, so to speak. The only good aspect of pride is when you feel it internally without anyone else confirming it. It is warm and almost post-orgasmic in the peace and tranquillity it brings. Everyone should experience internally that sense of well-done at least once in their life without anyone else around. It is far more satisfying than any award or compliment. One can never trust others who offer praise because it is impossible to know their motives for doing so, but one can always trust one's own inner true feelings.

Part 3: 2011 And The Future

19) Life After Work

"Immortality exists only in the thoughts of the living."

J. F. Sexton

It has been almost two years since I retired from the office. Some days I spend doing nothing which in itself is a radical departure from the a-type personality that I was. I have learned to enjoy sitting outside, sometimes even in the rain, nourished by the sights and sounds of nature, amused by the scurry of people passing by, and always comforted by my dog who wants nothing more than to know that I am there.

Other days, when I am inspired, I write things such as the material for this book or I putter about the house doing little jobs, and sometimes not so little jobs, that fix or improve this or that. I do those things not out of a feeling of obligation but out of a feeling that I want to make it better.

Perhaps that has always been my motivation, to make things better. But better is something subjective and always measured by those that are affected by the changes. When there is only myself, I find pretty much everything I do makes things better. But even now, I am seldom satisfied until I believe something to have reached the best that I can do. The many holes in the walls where I have re-arranged things until I felt they really worked for me are testament to that ingrained sense of perfection that I have never lost.

Even as I write these pages, I am contemplating re-arranging the desk in my office to make more efficient use of the space. After I retired, I purchased a number of tools and made room in the basement for an honest-to-goodness workshop. With those tools and my imagination, I have become a little bit of a designer and builder of things that make my life better. I took apart a small shelving unit that I purchased a few years ago and modified it to make it more compact and suitable to stack a number of electronic things on the periphery of my desk, thereby freeing a lot of desktop space. Now I am thinking that if I modify it again, I can add further space and make things look even more organized. I just do not know if I want to do that today or

151

maybe later. Such is the luxury of doing things for yourself. And just maybe I did learn something from living in Newfoundland all those many years ago.

I have been in limited contact with my old office. I have received a few calls and emails from them, mostly I suspect to re-assure themselves that they were still on track with the things I had wanted to do myself before I left. But I take comfort in the knowledge that things are moving forward and they are achieving tangible progress regardless of my presence. Knowing that your ideas have survived despite retirement is a tiny bit of proof that your ideas had value. It is a little like seeing your work remembered after death, if such a thing were possible. Knowing the people involved, I suspect they will take full credit for any success based on those ideas but that really does not matter to me since I know that such credit is short lived and must be constantly reinforced by other ideas that they may or may not be capable of generating.

I halfheartedly approached one of the local colleges about developing and delivering a course on the methodology that I felt best reflected my own way of critical thinking in business operations. They did not reply. It is their loss and makes no difference to me since my motivation was simply to share something of what I have learned and maybe inspire a young mind. But it may have been for the best in any case since it would have meant committing to another person's schedule and demands, something that I have grown to enjoy in its absence.

I still do not know what I want to be when I grow up. That may seem like a truly odd statement at this point in my life, but it honestly reflects my state of mind. I have never felt like I have found my final place in life. As I have written, my life has been one of happenstance not planning. I just do not know what may happen tomorrow, if anything at all. In some ways, I have always let others push or pull me along, seldom exercising a veto. It was only in my last two or three years of work that I set a course for myself and successfully pursued it. Now, in this phase of life, I am again rudderless but more content to be that way.

In youth, you are constantly being pushed to pick a career or just get a job. But there is positive motivation behind those doing the pushing since they want you to gain your independence and be a success. At work, if you do a good job there is pressure to move up the ladder. Again, there is positive motivation behind that pressure since all organizations need to constantly renew themselves with fresh talent.

I remember the impact that reading "The Peter Principle" had on my life. Sadly, I saw it in operation all about me throughout my life. There were many who rose quickly who I knew to be less intellectually capable than others in the office and when the principle kicked in, they got stuck at some point and quietly shifted out of the mainstream. I have to say that I always admired those that resisted what was expected of them in favour of what they really wanted to do. To me they had courage and were the real winners in life. It is not easy to defy all the pressure around you and set your own course. To place your own satisfaction above monetary reward is a wondrous but difficult thing.

Despite what you may have gleaned from reading this far, I have always been an optimist and capable of seeing the positive when everyone else sees disaster. I have never been able to live in gloom and have always been surprised by those that constantly dwell on the negative. It is better to find answers than to find problems.

But the reality is that most people worry about the problems in life and do not spend enough time solving them. Worse, they exaggerate the possibility of those problems becoming real and so become frozen like deer in a headlight, unable to take action to avoid catastrophe. That makes catastrophe all the more likely in a self-fulfilling prophecy.

While in the great span of time humans will cease to exist as do all species eventually, our individual lives are so short that it does not make logical sense to waste them. Embrace change that makes things better, challenge the *status quo* even at the risk of losing your place in it and really hear your critics when they make sense.

20) Things

"Humans view initial impressions with importance when, in fact, they almost always reflect our prejudices rather than reality."

J. F. Sexton

Things That Should Be Valued

In no particular order:

Simplicity

Simplicity is the key to all things. All concepts that begin in complexity end in disaster, because as any idea is turned into reality issues and problems arise. Thus, when the starting point is already complex, there is little hope for the future of that idea. When the starting point is elegantly simple and makes sense, then turning it into reality is almost always guaranteed. But the hardest thing to accomplish is simplicity itself. Simple is always challenged as being inadequate or as being just too easy to be right. The key to making simple work is finding the one big issue that appears to be in its way and overcoming it. The one entity that has truly mastered simplicity is the dog. It is content simply to be with its human companion and works hard to overcome its greatest obstacle, indifference, through any means bad or good.

Intellect

Finding someone who is capable of explaining concepts or things in a manner that is both thoughtful and understandable is rare. The ability to meaningfully translate notions to the level of understanding of a given audience is a gift. When tested, the intellect rises calmly to the challenge and answers with assurance. Over time, it always becomes clear if there is true depth of understanding at play or if what is being said is mere echo. The best test of this is when the questions reach the boundaries of understanding because the real intellect would admit with profound yearning that there is more to be discovered whereas the echo lacks that sense of yearning and only seeks to impress.

Time

It is said that time is the only thing that can be lost or wasted and never recovered. But time is never truly lost or wasted, it just continues to move forward and be consumed by the activities of the moment. Those activities always appear to be appropriate at that point in time and so ought not to be considered badly. According to Einstein, time can be distorted or used at differing rates, but it can never be recovered by the entity using it. Even if one goes back in time, the traveller will be the same age upon arrival as when the journey began and age normally from that point in time forward. Once time is used, it is gone. Therefore, it is important to value each moment whether it be in quiet solitude or in frivolous celebration. Time spent in solitude, alone with one's thoughts, is the most exhausting and must be balanced with frivolity to keep one refreshed.

Debate

To hear one's ideas challenged by thoughtful and factual debate is wonderful. There is nothing worse than hearing agreement from those whose understanding is minimal, or hearing disagreement from those who appear to be frozen in the *status quo*. Hearing nothing is, at best, neutral. Hearing questions is hopeful. But being challenged by real alternatives is the basis for growth. It is a true dialectic at work.

Logic

The ability to move forward by deduction is fundamental to being human. Logic's only fault lays in its foundation of assumption. One must assume something to arrive at a conclusion but one can never truly know if the assumption is correct even if the answer is proved correct. Much of human culture and knowledge has been based on assumptions which, over time, have been found to be incorrect. Logic is essential, but there is a true sense of accomplishment when existing assumptions can be proved wrong and, in doing so, provision is made for new answers.

Music

Music that challenges the body or the emotions is a wonder. If it fails to meet at least one of those objectives, it becomes dreary and an interruption. Modern trance music compels the body to move in rhythm to the beat, not unlike primitive tribal dance music. Music as toned background to meaningful and forceful lyrics can move people to tears of joy or sadness. To be successful, music must capture either the feet or the mind and keep them in captivity until it is finished. It is sweet imprisonment.

Nature

Nature has the innate ability to inspire awe and wonder. From the truly small to the impossibly grand, it is a marvel to digest. Humans are hopelessly attracted to the beauty of unspoiled nature, both violent and serene. But raw nature can be so overwhelming that it eventually pushes one away to pursue more mundane sensory pursuits. Like a brutal addiction though, it always pulls one back again, perhaps to a different spot, but always to the same need to be dumbstruck if only for a moment. Humans must have some deep need to go back to something real, not something built by their own hands.

Adrenaline Rushes

Many people seek out things that force the body into temporary states of fear because of the intense sensations brought about by the sudden release of adrenaline. Those sensations would normally be undesirable simply because adrenaline evolved as a response to crisis and no one wants to experience one for real. But because humans do not experience a life and death crisis often, they seem to have a need to create one just for the rush. Roller coasters, race cars, and many extreme sports are just a few things that humans have invented to replace the ancient fight for survival. It is a needed fix, a moment of uncontrolled terror in a controlled environment.

Real Friendship

So much has been written about friendship that it is difficult to add to that subject. But real friendship is rare. Real friends can be separated by distance and time but when reconnected it is as if the separation never happened. They do not have to explain any behaviour that would offend or drive others crazy. Faults are either invisible or are just part of who that friend is. Trust is absolute. A person is truly fortunate to have known more than a handful of people over a lifetime that have ceased to be acquaintances and have become real friends.

Things That Should Be Valued Less

Money

Money is one of those concepts that is truly artificial but has assumed an importance in most societies beyond its beginnings. To say that money is not important would be somewhat misleading. Money is important in the milieu of a money-driven society. It is of no value whatsoever where money does not exist as a concept. Primitive humans did not understand the concept of money. They knew only the concept of having enough to eat, shelter from the elements, and valued the skills and knowledge of their elders and craftsmen. Except in societies with a tradition of communal sharing, barter was the means to exchange goods and services. Over time, barter was replaced by money as a means to exchange fair value. It eliminated the need for complex three or four party negotiations to exchange goods. But once a person has enough to eat, good shelter and protection from the elements, all else becomes wants rather than needs. Modern marketing understands very well the power of generating wants where no needs exist. Today, all humans need enough money to live in basic comfort, but the definition of "enough" should not be exaggerated.

Things That Should Not Be Valued

"The Best"

Humans are constantly bombarded with the aspiration to have the best of everything. But is "the best" really necessary? Every product today is constantly changing, making "the best" a fluid concept demanding more and more investment to keep up. For the most part, "the best" simply means better appearance, added convenience, speed or less labour. That implies that one needs all those things. Is it important to obtain these things at some price point? What was life like before? Was it just fine or miserable? If a product is truly new and changes basic life, then it is probably worth investigating or purchasing. But if it simply makes some small improvement or looks better, then why should it capture people's imagination? Humans seem to have an irresistible urge to have the latest shiny bobble to prove in some way that they are doing well.

Things Learned From Others

The following are not exact quotes, but each conveys an idea. Some are profound, some are, in hindsight, outright stupid but each of these statements teaches or shows something, even when that lesson is in the negative, or what not to do or think.

- *"Keep your sense of wonder and exploration. Try to imagine how things work. Do not take things apart because you'll always end up with a piece left over when you put them back together. Use your head instead."*

    - from my father

- *"Let's go down that road and see what's there."*

    - from my father
    (who often detoured when the family was on a car holiday)

- *"Worrying about the future is never worth the sweat unless you can do something about it. And if you can do something about it, then get up off your butt and do it."*

    - from my mother

- *"Throwing away something that is not broken is wasteful and a sin."*

    - from my mother
    (who kept a drawer full of odds and ends that always found use)

- *"Women rode horses and they should drive cars too."*

    - from my mother
    (who never learned to drive having been forbidden by my father)

- *"Let other people tell you what you can't do."*

    - a Director
    (advising that one should never limit oneself)

- *"Life is what happens while you're busy making other plans."*
  - from the song "Beautiful Boy (Darling Boy)" by John Lennon
  (musician, composer and activist)

- *"Electrical Banana is bound to be the very next thing."*
  - from the song "Mellow Yellow" by Donovan
  (being sarcastic about new product marketing)

- *"Old folks will never use the Internet."*
  - a colleague in 1998
  (expressing an earnest assessment on the future of the Internet)

- *"Get out there and tell all of our field managers what's coming at them."*
  - a Director General in 1998
  (expressing an earnest assessment on the future of the Internet)

- *"I don't want to be first, but I hate being last."*
  - an Assistant Commissioner
  (expressing a common sentiment among most senior bureaucrats)

- *"All future change must conform to our current internal standards."*
  - an IT policy directive in 2009
  (trying to slow change by banning divergence)

Things Related to Human Behaviour

The following are observations made over a lifetime concerning the behaviour of humans interacting with each other. It is very likely that these things have been catalogued by some academic studying human behaviour and even given labels, but regardless they are things that are useful to know when dealing with other people.

"The Right Thing"

Humans always do what they believe is right. Sadly, the definition of what is right varies greatly from one person to another.

"The Shoes of Another"

One of the most difficult things to do is to put one's self into the shoes of another. While there is great value in understanding a partner, a friend, a neighbour, an opponent or an enemy, humans often fail in this task because they refuse to let go of their own motives and backgrounds which makes it impossible to think like the other person. In fact, most humans will interpret what they see and hear as reinforcing their preconceptions rather than making an objective assessment.

"Trends"

New things come and go. Many become very popular and trendy. This includes business practices and methods. But new things ought to be measured objectively by what they have the potential to contribute, not by how popular they become. Much energy and money is wasted keeping up with the trends.

"Focus"

It is impossible to focus on many things at once. At best, one can mentally file away thoughts about quite a large number of diverse things, drawing upon them when the time is appropriate. But to succeed, one needs to focus on one thing at a time until one's goals are achieved.

"Communications"

Never assume that anyone understands what has been said until they put those thoughts into action. Humans want to be seen as agreeable and are naturally shy to show their ignorance by raising questions. Therefore, they will almost always nod in agreement with statements that appear to be logical even if they do not truly understand them. It is even worse if they think they have an understanding but their actions prove subsequently that they do not.

"Errors"

Most humans dislike being proved wrong. They take such

failure as diminishing their person. Therefore, it is always unwise to tackle other people's errors head on. Instead, those in error ought to be given the means by which they themselves can change direction rather than being told to do so.

"Open Mindedness"

When one encounters a person who can freely admit to error without prompting, one can trust that person to have an open and progressive mind. To accuse that person of being indecisive or changeable would be a grave mistake unless they repeatedly change positions back and forth.

"Sincerity"

When gauging another person's sincerity, compare how that person behaves with a person of lower station to how that person behaves with someone of higher station. Are there similarities or differences? Does their behaviour change to suit what they believe to be desired by others? There will always be some things attributable to deference, but if the fundamentals do not change, then their sincerity is honest.

"Using People"

Some people will always seek to use others for their own benefit. There is nothing inherently wrong with either using others or being used provided that both sides fully appreciate what is happening, agree with the situation and can profit from it. Only when the agreement breaks down do problems arise.

"Trust"

Trust is the most valuable commodity between two people. When present, each can act independently without fear. When absent, every act generates suspicion, warranted or not. Trust flows from honesty and can be easily undermined by even the slightest untruth. Therefore, it is sometimes better to say nothing rather than lie.

21) A Little Bit More About Me

"Never depend on luck or fate, but always be thankful for its assistance."

J. F. Sexton

After bravely reading through this much about my life and my thoughts, I hope you will indulge me as I fill in some missing bits about myself.

I am an orphan of English, Scottish and Irish ancestry. It may seem odd to describe myself as an orphan, but both my parents are dead and those that have lost parents know how that feels. Normally, orphans are defined as children without parents, but when there is no one to whom you can retreat with absolute trust like your mother or father, you feel a degree of insecurity regardless of your age knowing that there is no one who will shelter you the same as they did. You move to the head of the line, the next to be a victim of that inherited and inevitably fatal disease called life.

I am a first generation Canadian of an immigrant parent. When I said that to a good friend, he looked very puzzled and finally said that I could not say that. I asked why. He answered that as an English Canadian and a member of the majority community, it was not right to claim to be the son of an immigrant. Again, I asked why the nature of my ancestry would deny me the right to that heritage and history. He looked flummoxed and repeated that it was just not right.

Stating the facts about my family's history and my heritage takes nothing away from anyone else. Why should being a member of the majority culture deny you the right to express your own background. Perhaps there is some social assumption that unless otherwise stated everyone has the same background and therefore talking about it belabours the obvious, becoming tedious. But I have always enjoyed hearing people's stories about their family's history because it says a lot, not about them necessarily, but about the environment in which they grew up.

I may speak about the inevitable end of life both for me as a person and for the species, but I am not fatalistic. It does make me sad, however, that all of my blood ancestors have now departed this world. The last of my parents' siblings passed away in 2009 just four years short of the one hundredth anniversary of my father's family coming to this country. I had been unable to attend many of the funerals of my other blood aunts and uncles, but I made a point to travel to this uncle's funeral to mark the passing of their generation. I went not because it was the right thing to do, but because I felt a deep undefined need to do it. Funerals are for the benefit of the living, after all, not for the dead.

At the service, I only recognized two cousins and their wives. I did not know any of the other mourners. But one woman came up to me after the service and said that she recognized my uncle's face in me. I really did not know what to say other than to thank her for saying so. She added solemnly that he was a good man, something that from a small town resident is high praise indeed particularly when said to a complete stranger who she will never see again.

I knew that my uncle, in addition to being a carpenter, was very active in his town working to save that which was worth saving. A newspaper clipping from 1998 talked about his efforts to save the old town hall which was almost 100 years old at that time and had served many purposes over the years, including being the first school for both him and my father. I remember him always speaking slowly and with purpose, carefully thinking about what he said. He had a sense of logic that was simple and straightforward. It was the type of logic that could typically stop salesmen or politicians in mid-speech with its piercing precision. Unless you had a very deep understanding of the subject, he could make you appear rather pompous or silly.

My uncle had no children by either his wife who passed away nearly 40 years ago or his second partner with whom he found happiness later in life. But about 30 people came to the graveside from a town of only a thousand on a Monday afternoon. If you scale that up comparing it to a funeral in a city of a million people like Ottawa, that is the equivalent of 30,000 attending on a working day.

I will not attract that many mourners.

Throughout my life, I have feared error. Errors that could affect myself were bad enough, but errors that could affect others caused me

164

great anxiety. Oddly enough, I have always truly forgotten the errors of others made in good faith unless, ignoring the lessons learned, they kept repeating them.

When I have actually made mistakes, I have beaten myself up over them often to the point of making myself sick. That is the legacy of parents focusing on the one low mark rather than the many high ones. There has to be a correct balance between fear of mistakes and false pride in success but I have yet to find it.

The one mistake that was made by another that I have never forgotten or forgiven was the behaviour of an emergency room doctor in a local hospital in Ottawa. I was seriously ill with a very high fever that had appeared suddenly and rose rapidly. The first doctor to see me was fairly sure that it was jaundice, or hepatitis, but not the type. But when the second, more senior physician, saw me, he said it had to be Hepatitis B because of my sexuality. I was desperately weak and fearing the worst. Then he muttered in the most condescending tone that I probably had AIDS as well. For the next few days, I was not only very sick but incredibly depressed. This was before the advent of the miracle drug cocktails that have allowed people to manage the virus. That doctor had passed a death sentence on me based on who I was, not on any medical evidence. After more than a week, it was determined that I had Hepatitis A, probably contracted from a contaminated food source when I visited Montreal. I did not have AIDS or even the virus that causes it. I can never forgive that doctor for the suffering he gave me based solely on his homophobic prejudice. He violated every principle of his caring profession without a thought and I suspect that to this day he is completely unaware of what he did and cannot, therefore, have learned anything from it. His behaviour was far worse than that of the pathetic drunken young man who left that vitriolic death threat on my computer.

I never thought that I had much of a sense of humour. I was never a good joke teller, and often found many jokes I heard to be lacking in humour, laughing anyway so as not to offend. But later in life, a number of folks tried to correct that opinion. In particular, several women working with me toward the end of my career commented on how I always made them laugh when the going got tough. They noted my uncanny ability to interject the one-liner that showed the absurdity of a situation.

I have never minded being made the butt of jokes, as long as I knew that the intent was not mean spirited. I learned to take it as the shy kid who was on the wrong end of many goodhearted jokes. But I have always tried not to make fun of anyone else out of fear that they might think I was being mean spirited to them.

Despite that fear of offending, I have always been quite cold, detached and determined in my criticism of ideas that I considered to be badly founded. I tried always to separate ideas from the person who articulated them because that is the essence of civil debate and progress, but my criticisms have not always been viewed in that light. Perhaps it shows through that sometimes I really have little patience for stupid ideas put forward by people who so earnestly believe in what they are saying that they block out any attempt to show the flaws in their logic. It is even worse to hear ideas promoted by people who do not believe in them but articulate them because some higher authority has asked them to do so. It would be better to hear that they were obligated to support something and thus were being honest, rather than to listen to them trying to genuinely advocate it as if it were theirs. Loyalty and obligation are very understandable, trying to create an appearance or impression is not.

Looking at myself candidly, it is true that I have always been able to find the silver lining in the darkest cloud. I do it instinctively. I am the epitome of that hated fellow of good cheer on the bleakest Monday morning. I will even admit to making fun of myself for having that image. Deep down, I do not think of myself as the eternal optimist, but I refuse to give in to pessimism without very good cause. My mind naturally looks for every possibility in every situation that might offer hope. And I seldom fail to find some bright spot.

I love animals and seem to have a natural gift of empathy with many of them. Even as a child when I was warned about approaching one particular dog who had a mean reputation, I quietly crept around, made friends with him and played with him without a care. Cats that have a reputation of being really picky about who they allow to pet them, almost always end up in my lap purring furiously. At an exhibition of farm animals, there was one magnificent tall stallion who was being pestered by everyone reaching out to touch him. He stood aloof. I patiently watched from the other side of the corral with some sympathy for his plight but noticed his glances from time to time.

166

When the crowd thinned, he gently came over to me and used his nose to nudge me several times. I think he was saying thanks for not bugging him, but then again, maybe he wanted me to go too. Even the wild animals I sometimes encounter in nature will often acknowledge my presence but not flee. I understand that if I make no threat against them and gently go about my business they will relax. I credit many animals with an intelligence that escapes most humans. They instinctively know who is a friend or foe. For them, actions count much more than words.

I have always yearned to be artistically creative. I took up photography because I had an aptitude to master the technology, even before digital photography, and so I only had to focus on things like composition to create better photographs. The camera did the painting, so to speak. Many of my pictures are of at least calendar quality although I still cannot claim to be a great photographer.

One younger colleague who accompanied me on a tour of our field offices commented that it was like being with Elvis. He noted that practically everyone who we encountered said hi to me by name. I had to disillusion him by saying that when you speak to many large audiences they remember you but you have little chance to remember them or their names. All one can do is say hi in return and smile. Appearing to be famous even in a small way can be deceiving and awkward. On the flip side, my experience was better than being shunned and forgotten.

I have always been a bit irritated by people, devices and systems that assume too many things about me. Take my name, for example. I am J. Frank Sexton, not John F. Sexton. However, I cannot be me to most modern computer systems. I have to adopt a first name, middle initial and last name format to please them. That is arrogance on the part of the programmers.

I have a personal dislike for computer operating systems and products that are designed to be idiot-proof. The companies that produce them make many assumptions about how you want to work and make it very difficult to change the software's assumption-based performance. That is fine for most folks and probably best for some. But I want to control my computer and how it functions without it giving me hassles in return. That is why I work almost exclusively on

Linux based computers and seldom use software that is made only for the most commonly deployed operating systems. Linux is free for everyone and has become very easy to install and use. It has retained its flexibility and can be configured any way I wish. It was designed to be network-aware from the ground up and is, therefore, much less vulnerable to the many threats present on the Internet. And most importantly, it is based on the open-source model of software licensing which is truly a remarkable advancement not only for computing but also for humanity.

I was not a collector of things when I was a child. But as an adult, I have accumulated a very large collection of pigs. The pig is a much maligned creature but it is highly intelligent. It is perhaps the power of its logic that permits it to wallow in the mud with great glee knowing that safety from the sun and the comfort brought to its skin is worth the appearance deficit. I have pigs made from practically every type of material known. I have pigs made from many types of metal such as pewter, brass, nickel and silver, including a set of very beautiful miniature *cloisonné* pigs from Japan. I have pigs carved from brushes. I have soap pigs, jade pigs, crystal pigs and several signed original creations in porcelain and enamel. I have a wooden Thai pig puppet. I even have a pig carved from a ham bone. I have pig clocks, a pig watch, pig salt and peppers, pig cream and sugars, pig boxes and a pig tureen, to name but a few functional items. In total, I have almost 2,000 pigs, mostly the cute plush type. But they were all acquired with fun and are kept with fondness.

22) The End

"Science is the means by which we seek to become better than our environment would otherwise have permitted and will be, therefore, our end."

J. F. Sexton

Recently there was a documentary on television which featured six well qualified men from science and journalism. Each of them felt that the world and the United States in particular was headed for catastrophe. Each identified a different way that catastrophe could unfold and each one was convinced that the end of civilization was looming. They talked about the end of oil, the end of clean water, nuclear destruction through an act or terror, the collapse of money itself or the growth of thinking technology, any one of which could devastate civilization. Near the end of the documentary, it dawned on the participants to ask themselves what would happen if more than one, or even all, of these events occurred at roughly the same time. What they did not discuss, however, was that all of these things have been made possible by humanity itself, not nature.

The species, *homo sapiens*, has experienced almost exponential growth in the last couple of centuries, a minuscule time span even for this planet. Science, particularly medicine, has immunized humanity against nature's tendency to keep everything in balance. But it is a natural law, nevertheless, that when species outgrow their sources of food and sustenance, nature always finds a way to re-balance life.

While Malthusian Theory may be largely ignored or discredited, there are increasing signs that the planet is being taxed to its very limits to sustain human life. For most of history, with some notable exceptions like the Maya and Sumerian civilizations, science and technology have come to the rescue as populations grew beyond their contemporary means of support. Science can make humans more productive, but when the elements required to sustain that increased productivity are finite, it begs the question about how long increased productivity will be the solution.

The oceans are clearly being depleted of the traditional fish

169

species upon which humans have fed for centuries. The hunting of wild animals on land for food became impractical quite some time ago, as did the gathering of wild fruits and plants. Humans now exist at the pleasure of corporations that make and distribute food.

But corporations, despite their publicists, are governed by the amount of profit they make not by any notion of civic duty. Corporate leaders understand that as populations grow, demand grows. In addition, corporations artificially create demand for new food products which did not exist in history. The combination of natural growth in demand and artificially created demand guarantees a bright corporate outlook, at least for the short term. But what about a century or a millennium from now?

The search for the raw elements that are being consumed with ever greater efficiency continues to go into previously unexploited lands, even under the sea, but this only emphasizes the finite amount of territory to explore. Can humans import the raw materials needed from other planets in this solar system? That is unlikely in the foreseeable future but even if it was, what about the finite supply of planets circling the Sun? Going to the nearest star, hoping that it has the needed resources, is eons away even given the exponential growth of technology.

However, the very thought of ravaging other planets sounds a lot like how a deadly parasite spreads.

Perhaps *homo sapiens* is nature's way of curing that rare infection in the universe called life. Humanity seems to be relentlessly and aggressively bent on wiping out all the other biological organisms existing on the planet. In only about half a millennium, it has already driven countless other species to extinction and has populated virtually the entire planet spreading its toxic waste almost everywhere.

Throughout time, balance has been the rule in the universe. When exceptions arise, they are vigorously dismantled by the forces of equilibrium. Over thousands of years, nature insists on maintaining that balance and has no hesitation to resort to violent means to restore it. It has no conscience, but it is driven by purpose.

As a species, it is certain that *homo sapiens* will cease to exist in due course. But humanity has been gifted with a brain that is capable of understanding itself and understanding the consequences of its actions. The real question is will humanity be capable of rising above its ruthlessly parasitic nature before its evolution to something else or extinction.

Do humans ponder about the organisms that died to provide the plastic packaging that is tossed away after most purchases? Do they wonder how many more organisms must die, and at what pace, to continue to provide those polymer chains? Plastic is an unsustainable product. Some of it can be and is being recycled, but most of it is jettisoned back into the environment where it will never give back its components to the planet. Matter and energy can never be destroyed, only converted. The plant and animal life that was transformed into petroleum and that science then transformed into plastic, now exists in a form that cannot easily be transformed into anything else thereby putting up another block against nature's balancing act.

But having no conscience, nature simply accepts what is happening and seeks to balance it with some other transformation, such as punishing the offenders by driving them into lifelessness like the plastic they created. If the predator destroys all the prey, then the predator will also die. If life seeks to destroy its own basis for living, then nature will allow it to happen. That is the balance of nature.

All humans have hope that society will stop ravaging the planet and finally understand the consequences of its actions. But most humans cannot help themselves as they plunder the resources around them. They are dazzled by what science has done for them and their lives and seldom have a second thought concerning what had to be destroyed to accomplish those things. Most predators kill to sustain themselves. Humans destroy to advance themselves.

The documentary on television cited earlier was made possible through electricity (created from oil and coal), water (to keep the participants alive), plastic in the television (made from oil) and US dollars (to pay everyone involved), all of which were claimed by the participants to be under threat. Did either they or the viewing audience feel any concern that they might be contributing to the problem? Probably not.

* * *

I wrote earlier that to criticize without offering an alternative is never constructive. Do I have alternatives to what our species is doing? Perhaps the most difficult thing to do is to step outside one's natural inclinations and try to think of alternatives to what we seem to be designed to do. It is also critically important to ask the right questions based on the right issues.

I believe that there are five fundamental problems for humanity.

The first is our real need to sustain life itself, that is by air, water and food. Without air we die in minutes. Without water we die in days. Without food we can last but a few weeks. Therefore, these things are truly precious and must be preserved and guaranteed.

Second is our need for energy to ease and improve our lives. Without energy, our lives would collapse. Even simple things like cooking require energy sources such as fire. Everything we manufacture requires energy as one of the fundamental inputs into the process.

Third is our need to recognize that the resources available on this planet are finite and there is a need to govern ourselves accordingly. Our explorations for resources have taken us further and further from where they are needed and used. There is only so much territory on this planet and there are more and more humans competing for the same resources.

Fourth is our need to recognize that we are truly just another species on this planet and have no right to extinguish other species upon which our own existence may depend. With every extinction caused by our actions or inactions, we continue to drive wedges into the fragile ecosystem. Sooner or later the odds suggest that one of those wedges will come back to haunt us.

Fifth, and finally, is the need to limit our own spread rather than nature doing it for us. It is very possible to attribute the cause of our other problems to our own numbers. We grow in population because we can, not because of any need to preserve the species.

Let us discuss each issue in turn.

Air, Water and Food

As a species, we are critically dependent on air, water and food. Therefore, treating these things with disdain must be thought of as a true crime against humanity. Every act, no matter how small or large, that puts toxic substances into our air or water risks lives. Every act, no matter how large or small, that eliminates or contaminates our food sources lessens our ability to feed ourselves.

No one ought to shrug off the importance of these three things.

Pumping substances into the air that, in sufficient quantities and densities, would kill or seriously harm should be severely punished. In the vast majority of cases, the entities doing this pollution are corporate but even the facade of a corporate entity must not allow people to hide from their responsibility to the species.

Pouring unused chemicals and even household cleaners down the drain increases the concentrations of those elements in our water systems and will eventually affect us all. Our society seems to be indifferent to the dumping of fatally toxic chemicals into the water as long as no one gets sick or no sickness can be traced back with certainty to those sources. The *laissez-faire* attitude we demonstrate to our precious fresh water supply is astonishing.

Our arable land continues to shrink because of urban sprawl in some places and desertification in others. The chemicals sprayed onto the soil, while boosting crop yields in the short term, may eliminate insects that are crucial to the food chain and may have long-term human effects not yet recognized.

Therefore, to protect our most critical resources, we must halt the continued dumping of unnatural substances into our air, water and land. Industrial by-products that are now jettisoned must be recovered and re-used. Household products must be biodegradable to ensure no inadvertent sources of toxins from the home.

Furthermore, as a species we must finally complete our transition from hunter-gatherers to consumers of domesticated food. That means an end to the industrial hunting of wild species which is now taking place on the seas. It also means an end to sport hunting and fishing. The only exceptions that ought to be permitted are for those small social groups that continue to exist primarily as hunter-gatherers and do not distribute the fruits of their labour commercially.

Energy

After air, water and food, the most important element in our life is energy.

All energy we use comes, directly or indirectly, from either gravity, the sun or the stars.

Fossil fuels are stored energy from the sun but are decidedly finite and it cannot be in our best interest to rely on these for much longer.

Hydro electricity is driven by the sun's recycling of water and the power of gravity causing the water to fall, but building dams disrupts our water supplies and destroys the habitats of other species.

Nuclear fuels are based on elements created by the fusion of atoms in the stars, but they are also finite and have very toxic effects on most species.

Geo-thermal energy is derived from the power of gravity compressing matter thereby generating heat. That source will eventually end as the heat generated is gradually lost to space. But at least it has a longer potential than fossil fuels.

The other gravity derived source of energy is tidal power. The tides continue day and night but building devices to capture the power of the tides would interfere with many marine species and human navigation.

Wind power is caused by the heating differential of the sun beating down on different parts of the planet. Wind drives both air and sea and can be harnessed either through air turbines or wave turbines. As long as the wind blows, wind can be an indirect source of energy without the sort of issues most other sources bring. But the wind is inconsistent over many parts of the planet and therefore cannot be relied upon to provide energy at all times.

Then there is solar energy which is derived directly from the sun. But the strength of the sun's rays hitting this planet varies greatly and happens only for about half the day in any given place. It is, therefore, nearly as fickle as the wind.

Finally, we have chemical energy which is created by the small batteries we use in various electronic devices. The elements that go into these batteries were created, like nuclear fuels, by the fusion of atoms in the stars. And like any other elements found on this planet, they are finite and some are toxic.

As a species, we must cease our reliance on the finite or toxic sources of energy we now use. We must focus on the long-term sustainable energy sources that we already know exist, wind and solar radiation. We must also continue the quest for new sources of energy.

However, the one major impediment to solving the energy problem is our inability to store energy in great quantities for long periods. Virtually all our current energy needs are consumed as we produce the energy. In other words, the electricity grid upon which we all rely operates in real time. If the source stops, the grid shuts down. That, by definition, represents a high risk to civilization no matter the amount of back-up plans.

If we look to nature, the human body stores energy very efficiently though the accumulation of fat. It is added when we do not need all the calories we consume, and used when we cannot consume enough food to replace what is required.

In principle, humans need the same ability with solar and wind energy sources. Once we harvest energy either from the sun or from the wind, we must be able to store it, not use it in real time. Humans are working hard on the development of batteries that are much more capable and efficient than what we have today, but nothing exists that can store energy in the sort of large quantities that our society requires to function 24 hours a day. However, it is this avenue of research that will be our salvation in the future.

In many ways, it is the same problem our human ancestors faced when finding ways to store surplus grain to create the basis for urban life. The discovery of how to preserve food over long periods was one of the key elements driving the change from a hunter-gatherer society to an urban society. Finding good solutions to storing large amounts of energy for long periods will bring about a similar fundamental revolution in our current way of life.

Can you imagine having a year's worth of electricity stored in your basement, harvested from the solar panels on your own roof and the wind turbine in your own backyard? Think of the changes that would make to society. No one would need nuclear reactors, gargantuan hydro-electricity dams, coal fuelled generators or the massive wiring that now links every home in the developed world. You could top-up your car from the basement instead of from the gasoline pump and never worry about another black-out. Your home could be heated and cooled from you own stored energy. It would be a dazzling revolution.

Our Finite Planet

Our planet is a finite size with finite resources. No matter how efficient we become in using those resources, no amount of wishful or creative thinking can ever change the sum of our planet.

Therefore, remembering that matter and energy can never be destroyed, we must ruthlessly pursue the development of products that are entirely biodegradable, re-usable or recyclable in some manner. In addition to eliminating the toxic substances that poison our air, water and food, we must eliminate every product, including its packaging, that is thrown away unless it is biodegradable. Non-biodegradable products and packaging must be collected once they are either no longer needed, broken or obsolete and all of their fundamental elements must be recovered.

Industry should be forbidden from extracting new raw resources unless it is clear that the pool of existing material will be insufficient. But in such situations, it should be mandatory that industry explore alternative materials that may be in abundance before being granted license to dig up more of our planet.

Remember asking the right question? Many societies express great angst about waste disposal, but that is not the real problem. The real problem is having waste to dispose.

Our Fellow Species

This planet is home to a vast array of life forms. Each has a place in a great ecosystem that we simply do not understand well enough to be tampering with it as we have.

No supernatural being gave humanity license to reign over the other creatures on this planet. We have great abilities and have become the top predator on the land, but that is not the same as having permission to wantonly destroy all other living things.

Great extinctions have occurred in the past and will continue in the future. It seems as if we are entering an era of great extinctions right now, but the cause is not external such as an asteroid. Humans are the plague. Without finding a way to co-exist with the other life forms on this planet, we risk our own extinction. The predator must eat, but only what it needs to survive. The things we view as pests are often the source of food for other species. Breaking the chain anywhere risks the whole ecosystem or, at the very least, puts pressure on it to adapt.

Under intense pressure to adapt, some elements will not be up to the task. Remember that most of the great whales depend on a food chain that begins with the smallest of life forms, plankton. Do we know upon what tiny species we depend?

Deliberately targeting any species for destruction, whether it is deemed a pest or not, must be stopped. If a species is a real or perceived threat to humanity, we need to re-think solutions to those perceived threats. Instead of spraying pesticides on crops, it would be preferable to develop new resistant plant species through traditional or genetic engineering. If certain species carry disease, the disease ought to be the target not the carrier. If wild plants, which we often label as weeds, encroach on our agricultural land, we should examine and mimic nature by fostering the plant's natural consumers rather than using poisonous herbicides.

While agricultural production may suffer somewhat, the absence of broad-spectrum poisons in our environment must be healthier for everyone. Furthermore, the reduction in food production need not be of concern if we solve the last and greatest problem, our own numbers.

Population

Thus we come to the last great issue. Our population is growing faster and faster and this cannot continue even if we solve the other issues raised above. Virtually all of our problems can be defined by the finite and closed nature of our planet. Being more clever in the use of resources does not mean they suddenly become infinite. And squeezing parts of the ecosystem to destruction by using up the planet's space is just as dangerous as hunting them to extinction.

Therefore, let us try to ask the right questions again. Do we not need to limit ourselves to a number that we, the planet and all the other living organisms on it can sustain in harmony, rather than seeking to sustain ever increasing numbers?

The notion of limiting our own species may sound naive or harsh, but it would seem to contribute mightily to the solution of the other issues as well. Having said that, it is unlikely that most humans would agree voluntarily to restrictions on their perceived right to reproduce. One need only to look at the policies of the People's Republic of China to see how people seek to avoid compliance with the "one child" policy. Asking them to do so as a matter of conscience for the benefit of the planet would be even less successful.

Therefore, there are few practical ways to achieve such limits.

My only suggestion is that society consider the carrot rather than the stick to control our population. Considering that humans have a deep need to reproduce, then perhaps they should be allowed to do so but only by obtaining the right to replace another human being.

To truly distinguish our species as being not only intelligent but more importantly wise, humans should be able to bequeath their "space" to another.

Nature balances most species by predation, disease, hunger and the failure of certain genetic changes. However, humanity is rapidly neutralizing these weapons in nature's arsenal at least with respect to itself. But the law of balance cannot be ignored. Therefore, should we not responsibly and humanely balance our own numbers without resorting to the evils of war or genocide? By defying nature's balance, we risk the perverse and ironic outcome that we are trying to avoid, namely extinction.

Let us examine the issues that could arise by establishing a legal obligation to obtain a "space" before having children.

For those in a position to bequeath their space, what might happen if they have no obvious person to whom they can bequeath their space. Others might want to bid for that space, thereby putting a monetary value on life. That may sound crass and immoral but it may, in fact, make life a more precious thing. Every life might have a very real and demonstrative value.

It may also lead to better behaviour on the part of prospective parents who hope to attract the attention of donors. Those prospective parents could have as many children as others grant them their space. Clearly that would be an incentive to demonstrate good parenting skills.

As a parent, imagine being able to grant your child the right to bring another into this world and imagine how profound a gift that would be.

It is also possible as a parent to imagine sibling rivalry for a bequest. It is not something that can be divided equally. But knowing the person to whom a bequest is made must improve the odds that the child will receive better parenting. And knowing to whom that life is owed must encourage a celebration of the donor's heritage.

However, the biggest benefit to this idea is that it is almost guaranteed to lower the total population of humans on this planet. If society were to deem the space left by individuals as void and non-transferable should they die intestate or die before reaching the legal age of consent, then inevitably shrinkage starts to take place. In addition, some humans will choose not to bequeath their space to anyone despite the social and monetary pressure to do so. And as population numbers start to shrink, most of our other problems become increasingly moot. It would be like waving a magic wand and having many of our problems shrink without really having to address them.

Looking at the negative issues, an evil person might want to extort a bequest and then kill the blackmailed individual to bring the bequest into force. However, the lack of immediate monetary gain as in an insurance scheme or estate inheritance makes the probability of such a scheme remote.

But the one issue that is most troubling about this suggestion is what to do about an unintended pregnancy that has not been granted a space. Religious issues aside, if the parent or parents wished to end the pregnancy then the problem is solved. On the other hand, forcing anyone down that path would not be desirable if they did not want such an outcome. Therefore, to resolve the legal issue, the government may wish to maintain a pool of spaces drawn from the deceased who did not allocate their space so that those spaces can be auctioned to parents of unplanned children. Alternatively, or in addition, the government may wish to maintain a registry of adults who possess the rights to one or more spaces but have been unable or unwilling to fill them. These space-holders could be matched to the unplanned children through adoption or they could voluntary transfer a space to the unplanned parents. Such a transfer would be an incredible gift of true goodness, kindness and charity. In any case, these options would maintain the population balance.

At the end of the day, though, it is probable that every religious organization, politician and entrepreneur will object in the strongest of terms to this suggestion. Religions will object because of their support for some god-given right to reproduce. Politicians will object because they can foresee a horribly negative photo-op with a weeping want-to-be parent who has not received any bequests. Entrepreneurs will object since growth would be made much more difficult when their markets start to shrink along with the population. In other words, every group with power or influence will block such a proposal.

It must be concluded, therefore, that our species does not have a bright outlook. We will fail by having no solution, and no desire to find one, to this last and greatest of problems.

Because we, as humans, are driven by hope, we refuse as a species to believe we could destroy ourselves simply by being who we are. We have faith that solutions will be found. But it is our very nature to be ambitious, driven by our brains, to find ways to become better. And today, becoming better means consuming greater and greater resources, albeit in more clever ways. We seem to be disposed to control our environment and do with it as we please, regardless of our level of understanding of the consequences of doing so. We have blithely reshaped this planet for about 4,000 years now. But our brains should be able to grasp that the uncontrolled and unplanned alterations to the planet that we are making are unsustainable. In the short space of 4 millennia, no one from that time could even imagine the place that the planet has become today.

When the lifespan of a species might normally be measured in millions of years, does any government or business have a plan for the next, say, four thousand years? What about the next one thousand years? What about the next one hundred years? No credible concern exists among the powerful for the future beyond what their imagination and ambition can see. And their visible horizon is very close, not like the vastness of the universe. Business makes plans and projections for the coming quarter, or 0.25 years. Governments draft budgets for the coming fiscal year and sometimes make projections for the next three years for a grand total of perhaps 4.0 years.

We put a price tag of "invaluable" on ourselves while we treat other members of the same species as commodities, not slavery per se, but as cheap fodder for industry and war. Capital moves to where it can be most effective in the procurement of inputs, workers being one of those. Nations seek ever greater access to resources and the most powerful of them do not hesitate to use force when existing resources are threatened. They treat lost humans simply as collateral damage. It is the very contradiction between seeing ourselves as invaluable and seeing others simply as cheap inputs to make life better that dooms humanity to be the parasite that it is.

Conclusion

It is often said that one cannot place a value on human life. But the planet has become aware that humans value their own comfort, security and lives far more highly than that of any other life form and higher even than other members of the same species. Humanity has put a price on all life that exists on this planet, thereby giving every species but itself an economic ranking in life's hierarchy. If you doubt that, just travel to your local marketplace and calculate how much a tomato is worth, or how much a puppy is worth, or even how much a rose petal that could be crushed for your perfume is worth.

To place a value on human life would be to understand finally how humanity is cheating the planetary marketplace. That marketplace will get its revenge. It always does. It is the law of balance.

Epilogue

"Humans are competitive by nature and seek reward, tangible or intangible, for virtually everything they do."

J. F. Sexton

I remember having a little chat with my last Director General shortly before I retired. I told her that much of my working life had been spent with my mind existing in an environment that was some three to five years ahead of the current reality. I tried to explain how difficult that had been at times when the people around me were often openly sceptical and critical. I gave her a paper I had written eleven years earlier that contained a proposal almost identical to something that was just being introduced. She was leaving for a trip to one of our field offices, but when she returned she told me that reading my paper on the plane was like looking into a crystal ball. She had thought about what I had said about mentally existing in the future and felt she understood the challenges that must have brought.

The civil service is not an environment where leadership through innovation is valued. That kind of leadership involves taking calculated risks which, in the private sector, can lead to great rewards. The civil service is a place where new ideas are assumed to be risky or dangerous unless it can be shown that someone else has done it already with success. It is assumed that new ideas ought to be introduced by the politicians who are ultimately responsible for the actions of the bureaucrats.

But this becomes something of a catch-22 when politicians have little experience operating a large enterprise which the bureaucracy has become and they themselves fear the consequences of any type of failure.

And so entropy sets in, energy is wasted and people become frustrated. This is one of the prime reasons that the bureaucracy is seen to be inefficient by the public. The bureaucracy is the last place to embrace change because they need to be absolutely sure nothing can go wrong that might embarrass the politicians.

A professional bureaucracy must exist to do the things that are demanded by the public. And it must be paid sufficiently to avoid the corruption so common in the third world. Politicians may rail against the cost and size of the bureaucracy but they all know that it is an inevitable consequence of meeting the public's demands for services. And every proposed cut to the civil service is met by some group's cries of being ignored or being treated unfairly. The bureaucracy must forever suffer the insults and stereotypes in silence, taking solace in the knowledge that they are doing the public's will as best they can.

For myself, I sat down one day a few months before retiring and started to calculate how much money I had saved the people of Canada over my career. It was a rather difficult calculation because savings are normally calculated only in the first year of change. But the reality is that if the change had not taken place, the cost would have remained on the books forever. The savings therefore ought to be calculated as a permanent reduction year after year until something else replaces it. Doing my arithmetic in that way, I calculated that my ideas had saved between $100M and $200M of taxpayer's money over my career. For that I received a nice computer signed and framed letter from the Prime Minister thanking me for my 30 years of service to the government and people of Canada. It is the same letter that every retiree receives when they leave.

I still think with some frustration about the things that I tried to do but could not accomplish during my career but those thoughts are fading with time. It has always been my plight to think about the misses rather than the hits.

When I look back, though, I accomplished far more than most people in my position. I remember meeting only a few others who were similarly innovation-minded and recall seeing them treated the same way that I was. Worse, I remember one individual who, unwisely in my opinion, accepted promotion to a position where he became a target and could not deliver his ideas. As a result he was demoted in disgrace. His real mistake was the belief that his new position brought enough authority to implement his vision on his own. There is no such position in the civil service.

Does all that make me bitter? Not really. Just as when I worked on an assembly line, I have kept my mind active and alert to block out the negative things around me. I look back with fondness at the many people I met, worked for, and who worked for me.

Those people, and the people of Canada who I ultimately served, are the source of the best memories of my career.

It is said that people ought to be measured not by their abilities but by their choices. By that standard many would say that I have disappointed, even failed, by choosing not to move up the executive ladder. But every other choice I made during my career was intended to make my small corner of the civil service more efficient for the benefit of the people of this country.

And by choosing to write this book, I have tried to bring the reader's attention to what I see as some of the very serious contradictions and problems of life all around us. It is only when the right questions are asked and when the answers are not assumed can we hope to solve our problems.